Escape from the Money Trap

Escape
from the
Money
Trap

Henry B. Clark

Judson Press, Valley Forge

ESCAPE FROM THE MONEY TRAP

Copyright © 1973

Judson Press, Valley Forge, Pa. 19481

Bible quotations in this volume are in accordance with the Revised Standard Version of the Bible, copyright 1946 and 1952 by the Division of Christian Education of the National Council of the Churches of Christ in the United States of America, and are used by permission.

Library of Congress Cataloging in Publication Data

Clark, Henry, 1930—
    Escape from the money trap.

    Includes bibliographical references.
    1. Christianity and economics. 2. Stewardship,
Christian. I. Title.
BR115.E3C56   248'.6   73-2610
ISBN 0-8170-0585-4

Printed in the U.S.A.

Contents

A
Word
from
the
Author

In the twenty-fifth chapter of the Gospel of Matthew we are told the followers of Christ will be judged by the way they have treated him as he has come to them in the poor, the humiliated, and the despised of the world:

When the Son of man comes in his glory, and all the angels with him, then he will sit on his glorious throne. Before him will be gathered all the nations, and he will separate them one from another as a shepherd separates the sheep from the goats, and he will place the sheep at his right hand, but the goats at the left. Then the King will say to those at his right hand, "Come, O blessed of my Father, inherit the kingdom prepared for you from the foundation of the world; for I was hungry and you gave me food, I was thirsty and you gave me drink, I was a stranger and you welcomed me, I was naked and you clothed me, I was sick and you visited me, I was in prison and you came to me." Then the righteous will answer him, "Lord, when did we see thee hungry and feed thee, or thirsty and give thee drink? And when did we see thee a stranger and welcome thee, or naked and clothe thee? And when did we see thee sick or in prison and visit thee?" And the King will answer them, "Truly, I say to you, as you did it to one of the least of these my brethren, you did it to me" (Matthew 25:31-40).

This book is Christian and biblically based. It is intended to be a guide and an inspiration for deeply committed people who really care about their brothers and sisters in need and about their own spiritual fulfillment in their Christian stewardship of economic resources. It will raise many questions about our economic system and about our values—values and attitudes about money and material goods as manifested in the way we spend our income, what we buy or want to buy, and what we consider worthy of our investment, building, and carrying out, individually and as a nation. This book will provide some guidelines for a Christian use of personal and family money and for Christian action to improve social structures and economic policies in the nation. It will offer some suggestions about better ways of using national resources so as to feed the hungry, clothe the naked, care for the sick, provide shelter to the homeless, and bind up the wounds of those who have been injured or cast aside.

Chapter 1 will help the reader to understand the meaning of the term "consumerism" as extreme, compulsive buying which becomes a vice and therefore the yoke of Mammon which is far more burdensome than the yoke of Christ (Matthew 11:30).

Chapters 2 and 3 will examine the American economic system in historical perspective. The premises and goals of the nineteenth-century market system will be contrasted with twentieth-century realities. This comparison, while affirming certain positive values, may serve to point out shortcomings of our present economic institutions and their operation, and some of the follies of our rich young nation.

In Chapters 4 and 5 we shall investigate the plight of the poor and the morally dubious favoritism enjoyed by the affluent. Poverty in this country is portrayed not as an unfortunate accident created by immutable laws of supply and demand, but rather as the result of a systematic blocking of real opportunities for the poor to advance themselves and the corresponding dispensation of privileges and advantages to those who are already on top.

Chapter 6 broadens the focus of the analysis of economic injustice by raising some questions about the international scene and ecological concerns which have to be faced.

Chapter 7 suggests a number of specific proposals for change in individual economic behavior in response to the needs described in the earlier chapters of the book.

Chapters 8 and 9 will be of particular interest to those who are deeply convinced of the need for new goals and policies on the part of economic, educational, and governmental institutions.

Chapter 10 returns to the personal focus with which the book began, as it asks, "What decisions have you reached during this study and what are you going to do about carrying them out?"

Some of these facts, interpretations, and suggestions may be difficult to understand or, in some cases, to accept and discuss. The reader may find himself protesting against the seeming one-sidedness of the diagnosis of an economic or moral sickness and the implications drawn from this diagnosis. He may feel that proposed solutions are often drastic or even unrealistic.

This book is offered simply as a springboard for study, discussion, reflection, and decision-leading-to-action, not as a compendium of perfect answers. All that the author can ask—and surely this can be fairly expected of Christians sincerely seeking a deeper understanding of the meaning of discipleship in our time—is a willingness to consider openly and seriously the ideas that are presented, even those ideas that are startling, unsettling, apparently uncalled-for, or in any way threatening.

The struggle for economic justice is both more hopeful and more difficult than ever before in the history of mankind. On the one hand, the technologically advanced nations now have the means to eliminate almost entirely many of the economic ills which have always plagued mankind. On the other hand, it is more perplexing than ever for individual Christians, or groups of churchmen in the same community or vocation, to know exactly *what to do* to realize the promise of our economic and technical abilities.

Because of the interdependence of modern life—in which the carelessness, perversity, or even simply the misfortune of one person can cause so many difficulties for so many others—it is more necessary than ever for the citizens of a community, a nation, and ultimately the entire earth, to try to understand and respect each other as deeply as possible and to be willing to live with a greater variety of opinions and styles of life.

This means that all persons must be willing to work harder than they have ever thought possible in trying to understand economic matters which often cannot be understood easily. We must struggle more courageously to gain the experience and the wisdom that will enable us to be more effective in changing our economic system so that it does what God wants it to do. We must engage each other honestly and tenaciously, seeking the truth, and being open to it even when it hurts, confident that if we can speak and hear the truth in Christian love, it will set us free to be better stewards (Ephesians 4:15). Yet we must not be unfairly suspicious of, or afraid to be, "troublers in Israel," for that is what the prophetic voices of God's people have usually been called, on first hearing (see 1 Kings 18:17 and Amos 7:10-13).

1.
"Consumerism," the Yoke of Mammon

Let us begin our study of the Christian stewardship of economic resources by asking ourselves this question: What have I spent my money for? To experience the implications of the question, go, or imagine that you are going, to a place in your home where you are surrounded by the material possessions you cherish most dearly. If the living room is your pride and joy, look around at every prized article of furniture—the color TV, the stereo, the piano, or the sofa. Think about how long it took you to save up the money to buy the wall-to-wall carpet—or how long it will take you to save enough to get the carpeting you need to make the room just the way you want it! Remember how much *time* you spent deciding on each big purchase, hunting for just the right item, and finding just the right place for it in the room.

Or look out the window at the garden, the car, the camper,

the boat, the power lawnmower—or whatever it is you value most highly, whatever you have spent the most time in obtaining or caring for. Recall the sacrifices you had to make in order to get what you have, and enjoy honestly and unabashedly the pride and satisfaction you felt in having been able to attain your present state of comfort, however modest it may seem to you.

If you live in the city, think about the neighborhood in which you have chosen to live. Perhaps it is an expensive in-town apartment house. Recall the cost and the struggles you have faced in making this dream come true.

Now open your purse or wallet and take out some money. Look at it closely. Feel it. Consider how remarkable it is that these little pieces of paper can serve as tokens of exchange value which enable men and women with diverse talents to trade their labor for the products of the labor of other people whom they never know or see. It's a magic kind of paper, and we don't find it hard to understand why a lot of people have, for all practical purposes, fallen in love with money.

As you finger those greenbacks, think how drastically their exchange value has fallen with the rising cost of living in recent years. You are a very lucky person if inflation has not made a mockery of some of your long-range spending plans. Experience deeply, now, the anxiety you feel as you worry about the future impact of inflation: Will the retirement income you have worked so hard to set up keep you alive when the time comes, or will the savings set aside for the education of your children really suffice for that purpose?

If your mood has changed a bit from comfort and satisfaction to mild anxiety, you are ready for the next step in this exercise.

Leaf through some newspapers and magazines filled with

ads and feature stories that keep giving you new ideas about additional possessions and pleasurable experiences for which you might develop a desire. The illustrations in *Better Homes and Gardens* or *House Beautiful* will reveal how far you still have to go in furnishing and decorating your home. The fashion ads will make the wardrobe in your closets seem pitifully limited. The travel pictures will make your two-week camping trip last summer seem rather dull. A variety of ads and stories on insurance or education may make the principal breadwinner of the family positively *frantic* about the insufficiency of the security planning for his or her dependents.

Reflect, now, on the gamut of emotions you may have just run through. Have you given yourself time really to *feel* them? Is your reaction one of apathy or despair, a sense of defeat at your inability ever to "get ahead" or be firmly established in the promised land of eternal economic security?

Is this the way it's always going to be? Will satisfaction be followed by dissatisfaction when you compare where you are with how far you think you still want to go—followed by depression, frustration, and even anger when you realize you just can't win in the great game of consumerism? And what's more, you can't even count on the respect of those, perhaps your own children, who may have decided not to play the game. Is this not a vicious cycle?

One way out, of course, is to ask yourself what is your basic stance in life. Do I really want and really enjoy all these prized possessions I've worked so hard to obtain or am still working for—the furniture, the clothes, the car, the color TV, the apartment? How much genuine satisfaction do I really get out of them? Am I becoming a slave to things? What is really valuable to me? And what is just superficial?

Are these things really worth the price I have paid and the demands they continue to make upon my thought and energy? Or have I perhaps been sold a bill of goods by clever advertising?

Many of your possessions and pastimes can stand the test. Many products on the market do help persons find fulfillment and a kind of liberation. They are not all bad, if used properly. Few things are evil in themselves, and many are good if they contribute to personal fulfillment and are within a context of social and economic justice.

But it is "consumerism" which is wrong, that process of continual striving for more and more, the treadmill of always having to earn more in order to buy more. This extreme, compulsive buying does indeed become a vice. This is the yoke of Mammon. This is what makes it necessary to spend time moonlighting which could have been better spent with your family or in other constructive ways.

For the Christian, the answer to many of these questions may be found in a study of a few passages from the Bible.

What is the message in Jesus' parable of the prodigal son (Luke 15:11-32)? What would it mean if we "came to ourselves"? Could it be that we would know that we have wandered afar and wasted our substance on culturally stimulated forms of riotous living which offer no true satisfaction or joy in the deepest sense?

The prophet Micah described some unfortunate sinners in this graphic way:

> You shall eat, but not be satisfied,
>   and there shall be hunger in your inward parts;
> you shall put away, but not save,
>   and what you save I will give to the sword:
> You shall sow, but not reap;
>   you shall tread olives, but not anoint yourselves with oil;
>   you shall tread grapes, but not drink wine.
>   Micah 6:14-15

The prophet Jeremiah rebuked the people of his time for "[changing] their glory for that which does not profit," lamenting their folly in this memorable image:

> for my people have committed two evils:
>> they have forsaken me,
> the fountain of living waters,
>> and hewed out cisterns for themselves,
> broken cisterns,
>> that can hold no water.
>
> Jeremiah 2:13

It is sobering to ponder the message of the biblical prophets for present-day Christians. Are we not involved in a similar folly, which deserves the same sort of rebuke? In allowing ourselves to waste our attention and our energies on the never finished, never fulfilling, and ultimately exhausting treadmill of "consumerism," are we not duplicating the pitiable error of Esau in selling our spiritual birthright for a mess of pottage (Genesis 25:29-34)?

To put the argument in terms of a familiar verse from the New Testament which is particularly appropriate in this connection, the blessedness of serving God ought to be easy to embrace when we consider the sorrows and horrors of being enslaved to Mammon (Matthew 6:19-21, 24). Serving Mammon instead of God, or laying up treasures on earth instead of heaven, is foolish as well as wicked. To be delivered from such futility and such faithlessness is to be restored and made whole, not to be denied anything worth having. The yoke of economic sanity and justice shouldered by the twentieth-century Christian who rejects consumerism is indeed easy and light (Matthew 11:30) in comparison with the burdens he must carry if he is "hooked" on the drugs of the mass-consumption society. Nothing is worse than the ever deepening despair of the comfort/status addict who carries the ever heavier and more intolerable weight of his own pride and anxiety, which may indeed be symptomatic of his sinfulness.

Let this thought really sink in—is it possible that consumerism is enslavement, and abandonment of it is liberation? Perhaps we should think of the false values of consumerism as demons which the power of Christ in our hearts will drive out (see Luke 10:17-18). Such an experience can still happen today. It *must* happen if we are to enjoy rightly and meaningfully the goods of this life which God has put at our disposal.

2.
Christ
and the
Rich
Young
Nation

Pick up a newspaper, or if it's close to the time of a full-length TV news report and analysis, listen to that. The chances are you will read or hear a number of stories having to do with huge federal expenditures for such things as highways, military weaponry, or space projects. In the financial section of the newspaper you will learn of shifts in the value of various stocks in response to recent research breakthroughs, investment decisions, and profit statements of major corporations. You may even discover that something important is happening in the economic affairs of your own city or state: a new plant being opened (or an old one being closed down), a report of increased pollution levels in the water or air, or the latest figures on wages and prices and their effect upon the cost-of-living index.

The mere magnitude and complexity of some of these

matters may bring a sigh of bewilderment, if not a surge of indignation, about the amount of money that is involved. Actually, most of us are tempted to give up thinking about public affairs and turn to the sports page of the paper or the comedy show on television. But as citizens of democracy we do have opportunities to influence the policies carried out by institutions for which we work, associations to which we belong, and the various levels of government. Thus, we have a responsibility to be as well-informed as possible in order to form a decision about what needs to be done, and what we personally can do in regard to particular issues.

Consider now, for a moment, the information you have read or heard. Exactly what will we as a nation have when a certain federal expenditure is made? What good will it do us and/or other members of the human community in other countries when we have it? What effect will this expenditure have on our ability to pay for certain other projects and programs that are greatly needed? Which segments of our population will be served, and which segments will be deprived, by the expenditure in question? And what will be the consequences of this particular project, both in terms of depletion and pollution, on our supply of natural resources?

Questions of this kind must be answered if Christian stewardship of *national* resources is to be adequately practiced. For economic injustice can be created and perpetuated on a massive scale when it is built into the *system* of accepted practices—what is seen as fully legal and "normal"—in a whole nation or among a group of nations operating in international trade.

Examine the following examples:

 • We can easily see the wickedness of the *individual* who is obsessed with making as much money as he possibly can regardless of how he does it, the man who cares most of all in life about his bank balance and watching it grow. We condemn the moral blindness of such a man and the sins of dishonesty and callousness of which he is probably guilty. We also pity his shortsightedness. Is he not like the rich man whose soul was required of him just as he was in the act of eating, drinking, and being merry (Luke 12:16-21)? Shouldn't we feel the same mixture of blame and sadness at the sight of a *nation* which measures its economic success too exclusively in terms of its growing gross national product (GNP)? After all, the GNP is nothing but a figure arrived at by adding up the sum of all economic activities which create value in any product that is raised or manufactured and sold. It shows only the *quantity* of monetary value generated; it reveals nothing about the *quality* of what is produced and marketed; and it tells us nothing about the importance or the triviality of these commodities and services.

• We can spot the immorality and foolishness of an individual's preoccupation with gadgets and gimmicks, fashions and fads, and the whole range of assorted goods and goodies advertised as necessary for the "gracious living" that all Americans are supposed to want and spend their money to obtain. But isn't his foolishness comparable to that of a nation which cannot resist spending huge amounts of tax revenues for "the latest thing" made possible by technology? Although it is not quite true to say that "anything that *can* be done by technology *will* be done," there is certainly a tendency on the part of many scientists, engineers, corporation executives, and government officials to want to experiment with the actual development of any exciting new technological toy that has been proven theoretically possible through research.

• We also can readily spot extravagance on the part

of an individual. We usually have in mind that he is living beyond his means. Sometimes, however, we mean that he is mis-allocating whatever resources he has by spending money for certain things he doesn't really need and is neglecting to supply his family with other things they do need. A nation may also be guilty of the same faults. It may deplete seriously its resources, either by ruining them with pollution or by using them up so recklessly that posterity in the not-so-far-off future will not have a supply of them at all. Or it may invest resources in relatively useless or destructive purposes at the expense of the citizenry, especially certain groups of citizens, who are not provided with essential goods and services. These citizens may not have sufficient economic or political power to make their voices heard.

THE *CALLING* OF AN ECONOMIC SYSTEM

We should be able to speak of the *vocation*, the *calling*, of an economic system (or of its main institutions and the people who run them) in very much the same way as one speaks of the calling of an individual. This idea will be sketched in greater detail in the following chapter, but the main point should be familiar to Christians: God has ordained certain "orders of creation," such as the state, the family, and the economy, which are charged with the responsibility of caring for some crucial area of human need. If this classical theological notion is taken seriously, the economic system of America does not merit a very high mark for faithful performance of its vocation. As technologists such as Seymour Melman, economists such as John Kenneth Galbraith, and moralists such as Michael Harrington are continually proclaiming, there is an outrageous discrepancy between the capabilities of our marvelous technical machinery and the output and distribution of goods flowing from it.[1] The affluent society is glutted with superfluous products which we are manipulated into wanting by the hidden persuasion of advertising, while at the same time there exists alongside it "the other America" of the poor who lack all kinds of basic necessities. And both segments of the population suffer from a lack of adequate *public* goods and services—hospitals, schools, sanitary facilities, public transportation, and the like.

Most of us would not say that *all* expenditures for military hardware are unnecessary, although of course some Christian pacifists would say that all such expenditures are morally wrong. Some would not even contend that the vast sums allocated for the military-industrial complex and the highway-industrial complex are self-evidently extravagant, although many observers have gone so far as to make this assertion.[2] But we do need to make a very sober reconsideration of the desirability of these expenditures in the light of an honest assessment of the actual benefits purchased. The assessment must be made, of course, with full consideration of *other options* in science, defense, transportation, and public needs in general—particularly the needs of the poor, who have no powerful lobbies representing their interests in the appropriations committees of Congress or the executive agencies in Washington.

The implication is, to be sure, that some of these high-priced items are unnecessary or dangerous, and therefore

[1] See Seymour Melman, *Our Depleted Society* (New York: Holt, Rinehart and Winston, 1965); John Kenneth Galbraith, *The Affluent Society* (Boston: Houghton Mifflin Company, 1958), and Michael Harrington, *The Other America* (New York: The Macmillan Company, 1962).

[2] Fred J. Cook, *The Warfare State* (New York: The Macmillan Company, 1962), pp. 175-213; Seymour Melman, *Pentagon Capitalism: The Political Economy of War* (New York: McGraw-Hill Book Company, 1970).

undesirable. From a Christian perspective there are three implications which are especially important:

1. Hospitals and schools ought to be built before electric toothbrushes and rockets to Mars.

2. National resources ought to be conserved and kept reasonably uncontaminated for use in meeting real human needs instead of spurious uses.

3. Technological research and development ought to be focused on human welfare and fulfillment rather than governmental domination or corporate profits.

The sinfulness of the individual who serves Mammon and not God (Matthew 6:24) is compounded a thousandfold in the nation whose economic system is guilty of sins of commission as well as the above-mentioned sins of omission. The failure of our economy to live up to its calling is not simply the result of heedless use of resources to meet consumer demands (real or fabricated, basic or superfluous), or the consequence of the mere mis-allocation of energy and goods. Is the failure not also caused by a system of institutional policies and individual rewards and punishments that result in outright exploitation of the poor in this country and abroad?

In its least virulent form, the system works simply to draw money and trained personnel away from areas of high priority need into areas of lesser need. Two illustrations will suffice to make the point clear.

1. We would condemn the individual doctor who refused to live up to the Oath of Hippocrates by declining to give medical treatment to a needy person simply because that person couldn't pay for it. But the real problem of medical care in a country like the United States is not the greed or lack of concern of individual doctors. The problem stems mainly from a medical-care *system* which insures neglect of the

poor. It keeps the number of trained medical personnel artificially low by restricting the building of medical schools and admissions to them. It allocates research funds to glamorous frontier issues that are not likely to benefit large numbers of persons any time soon instead of to the problem of extending basic medical care to all those who do not currently have it.[3] It gives the highest payoff to specialists, making it financially and administratively difficult for a doctor to be an old-fashioned general practitioner.

2. The 1949 Housing Act, through authorization of the construction of public housing, made a theoretical commitment to provide a decent place for every American to live.[4] Only a fraction of the money necessary for the accomplishment of that objective was ever appropriated, and millions of poor citizens have been forced to live in rat-infested tenements ever since. But many times the amount of money needed for housing has been appropriated for the nation's elaborate interstate highway system. Thus middle-class citizens have an easy way to get to their vacation homes or to resort areas on weekends or at vacation time, while poor people have more pressing needs that remain unmet.

The greatest and most serious portion of economic injustice in the contemporary world is the portion caused and perpetuated by economic and political institutions and the social structures supporting them, not by the isolated vices of individuals. The bulk of the problem comes from what we call "normal" and "legal" behavior, not from what is generally considered criminal behavior. If this is so, the solution to economic injustice depends mainly upon reform of these "normal" structures and institutional practices. The

[3] Anne R. Somers, *Health Care in Transition: Directions for the Future* (Chicago: Hospital Research and Educational Trust, 1971).

[4] Michael Harrington, *The Other America* (New York: The Macmillan Company, 1962), p. 139.

crux of the matter is not the dishonesty of unscrupulous men, but rather *the conscientious performance of able, diligent men who run economic machinery that does a very efficient job of dehumanizing and oppressing countless millions.*

Christian stewardship of economic resources in this century must include knowledge about and attempts to reform some economic institutions and practices that we have been conditioned to think of as right and fair.

This emphasis on the national counterpart of unfaithful stewardship is important for two principal reasons. The first is *that the lives of so many individuals are affected* by patterns of injustice which have become accepted as "business as usual" in retail stores, banks, factories, executive suites, and government offices throughout the country. The second is that popular Christian piety in its stress on personal ethics has often tended to overlook collective sin and the need for reform of institutional policies. Unless the significance of *collective* sin in economic *institutions* is appreciated, the Christian witness in the economic area will be sadly incomplete, and Christian action to implement God's will in economic life will be pathetically ineffective. For every person who is cheated by a deliberately dishonest swindler, or edged out by an unreasonably avaricious competitor, a dozen are deprived and exploited by the everyday operation of economic machinery that runs smoothly because it is efficiently manned by polite, well-meaning, honest, conscientious persons who do not know what evils they are perpetrating or who have never had the incentive to investigate.

A BIBLICAL PERSPECTIVE

It is surprising as well as tragic that Christians have so

often neglected this elementary fact of life, for the Bible and the church have never ceased to emphasize the social nature of the gospel of God's grace and his will for the human community, and the need for God's people in the household of faith to take thought together and act with a disciplined common commitment to bring about economic justice.

When the Old Testament prophets excoriated "those who add field to field, until there is no more room" (Isaiah 5:8), they were reminding the real estate operators of their time that sharp dealing, even if successful, was wrong when it unjustly displaced fellow members of the covenant community. When they condemned those who have "the spoil of the poor . . . in your houses" and those who "grind the face of the poor" (Isaiah 3:14-15), they were indicting prosperous merchants whose prices were probably reasonable in terms of contemporary notions of the law of supply and demand, which allows whatever price the market will bear.

They issued warnings in the name of the Lord God of hosts to the proud:

> Woe to those who are wise in their own eyes,
> and shrewd in their own sight!
>
> Isaiah 5:21;

warnings to the drunkards:

> Woe to those who are heroes at drinking wine,
> and valiant men in mixing strong drink!
>
> Isaiah 5:22;

and warnings to the lovers of luxury:

> The daughters of Zion are haughty
> and walk with outstretched necks,
> glancing wantonly with their eyes,
> mincing along as they go.
>
> Isaiah 3:16.

When these warnings were issued, they were pronouncing God's judgment not only upon the sloth and the indulgences of rich individuals, but also upon the whole set of cultural standards which made this unworthy behavior pattern symbolic of success and status (see Amos 6:4-6).

When they heaped curses upon the heads of dishonest public officials,

> You who afflict the righteous, who take a bribe,
>   and turn aside the needy in the gate
>   Amos 5:12; cf. Isaiah 5:20,23

they were rebuking not just a few iniquitous individuals but the "smart way of doing business" or "getting along by going along" characteristic of economic and political life in eighth-century Israel and seventh-century Judah. They were pointing out the hypocritical shallowness of a revival in which emphasis upon religious ceremonies cloaked impatience to get back to the lucrative commercial dealings of Monday morning:

> Hear this, you who trample upon the needy,
>   and bring the poor of the land to an end,
> saying, "When will the new moon be over,
>   that we may sell grain?
> And the sabbath,
>   that we may offer wheat for sale,
> that we may make the ephah small
>   and the shekel great,
>   and deal deceitfully with false balances,
> that we may buy the poor for silver
>   and the needy for a pair of sandals,
>   and sell the refuse of the wheat?
>   Amos 8:4-6

The teachings of Jesus are usually interpreted as *personal* admonitions in view of his concern for a recovery of personal holiness in the wake of pharisaical legalism and the upheavals of the Roman conquest. But is it not reasonable to suggest that there is a general ethical commandment which applies to *institutions* and *nations* in such passages as the parables of Lazarus and Dives (Luke 16:19-31) and the rich young ruler (Mark 10:17-22)? Above all, the description of the Last Judgment in Matthew 25:31-46 must be seen as an announcement that generous sharing of oneself and one's substance *beyond all culturally defined criteria of what is normal, lawful, reasonable,* or *enough* is required of those who take up their cross and follow Christ. The early church had a lively realization of this point, for the earliest Christian communities provided for all of their members by means of what sociologist of religion Ernst Troeltsch called the "Communism of Love."[5] "There was not a needy person among them, for as many as were possessors of lands or houses sold them, and brought the proceeds of what was sold and laid it at the apostles' feet; and distribution was made to each as any had need" (Acts 4:35).

Unfortunately, the doctrine of social solidarity characteristic of the Bible and the early church has been largely lost in the subsequent centuries of Christendom, particularly since the rise of Renaissance individualism and the Industrial Revolution.[6] But surely we should be well aware today that the full gospel includes a social gospel, that concern for salvation in the next world must be accompanied by concern for justice and love in the human community right now. Because sin is collective and systematized in the structures and processes of society, goodness and evil must be understood at the societal level as well as the personal level. Transformation must take place in society as well as in

[5]Ernst Troeltsch, *The Social Teaching of the Christian Churches* (London: George Allen & Unwin, Ltd.; New York: The Macmillan Company, 1931), p. 62.

[6] For an account of these historical developments, see Henry Clark, *The Christian Case Against Poverty* (New York: Association Press, 1965), pp. 14-67.

persons. As Walter Rauschenbusch proclaimed, the mission of the church in modern society includes endeavoring to "Christianize the social order."[7]

But many good Christian people who understand all of this often do not seem to realize that what is true of the *goals* of ethical endeavor is equally true of the *means* by which transformation is sought. Many staunch Christians may be under the illusion that social change will come about more or less automatically if enough individuals are changed in their hearts, one by one.

But the darkness of this sinful world cannot be effectively illuminated by the lighting of individual candles, here and there. Those who seek to illuminate some area of darkness can accomplish this purpose best by getting together with like-minded people and building a dynamo to provide adequate, permanent incandescent lighting for everyone! Penetrating, long-lasting transformation of the structures of society requires the coordination of resources and efforts into a *strategy* of social change at the institutional, local, state, and national levels. Effective strategy planning requires detailed knowledge of how the present social system works, so that its virtues can be preserved and its weaknesses remedied. Therefore, the next few chapters of this book are given to an examination of the way our present economic system functions and of some of the moral questions raised by the resulting analysis.

[7] Walter Rauschenbusch, *Christianizing the Social Order* (New York: The Macmillan Company, 1926).

3.
Does Our
Economic System
Live Up to
Its Best
Possibilities?

The purpose of this chapter is to reexamine the widely held notion that the American economic system is doing *the best job possible* in meeting the needs of its people sanely and equitably. The question is: How can our system be improved and made just? Michael Harrington has expressed the point eloquently in his statement about the poor in *The Other America:*

> What shall we tell the American poor, once we have seen them? Shall we say to them that they are better off than the Indian poor, the Italian poor, the Russian poor? That is one answer, but it is heartless. I should put it another way. I want to tell every well-fed and optimistic American that it is intolerable that so many millions should be maimed in body and in spirit when it is not necessary that they should be. My standard of comparison is not how much worse things used to be. It is how much better they could be if only we were stirred. [1]

[1] Michael Harrington, *The Other America* (New York: The Macmillan Company, 1969), p. 18. (Copyright © Michael Harrington 1962, 1969.)

NINETEENTH-CENTURY IDEOLOGIES

John Maynard Keynes, the great British economist, whose theories were instrumental in helping many governments solve the problems associated with a fluctuating business cycle during the twentieth century, once remarked that ideas—specifically, ideas from the history of economic theory—are far more important than is generally acknowledged. He even claimed that "practical men, who believe themselves to be quite exempt from any intellectual influences, are usually the slaves of some defunct economist. Madmen in authority, who hear voices in the air, are distilling their frenzy from some academic scribbler of a few years back."[2] The point is doubtless exaggerated, but the one compelling example of Keynes' thesis is the eighteenth-century Scottish philosopher-economist, Adam Smith. Smith's almost literally earthshaking work, *The Wealth of Nations,* put forth the doctrine of "the invisible hand" that inaugurated the reign of what we have come to call "the free-market system."[3]

The theory of the invisible hand is one of the most optimistic messages ever proclaimed to mankind. It asserts that individual selfishness in the economic arena is no vice, for each individual's effort to make the most profitable use of his resources will also lead to the best use of those resources for society as a whole. In seeking his own financial advantage

[each individual] intends only his own gain, and he is in this, as in many other cases, led by an invisible hand to promote an end which is no part of his intention. . . . By pursuing his own interest he frequently promotes that of society more

[2] Quoted in Robert Heilbroner, *The Worldly Philosophers* (New York: Simon & Schuster, Inc., 1953). pp. 4-5.

[3] For a stirring account of the main ideas and the enormous significance of *The Wealth of Nations,* see *ibid.,* pp. 42-66.

effectually than when he really intends to promote it. [4]

Moreover, Smith thought that allowing the market to operate freely—allowing the "laws of supply and demand" to determine production, prices, wages, and the location of factories, distribution centers, and retail outlets—would make the average consumer undisputed king of the realm. He thought that the condition of the common man would keep on improving indefinitely as a result of "the tremendous gain in productivity which sprang from the minute division and specialization of labor" fostered by the free-market system.[5]

Needless to say, this message was particularly welcome to "the nation of shopkeepers," as eighteenth-century England has been called, and to entrepreneurs all over Europe at the time of the Industrial Revolution. The free-market system worked very well to facilitate the geographical and commercial expansion of the next 150 years. Small wonder, then, that Smith's theory has become enlarged upon and refined into the full-blown ideology of capitalist society.

The assumptions underlying the free-market system and the claims advanced to explain its preeminence as an economic philosophy are summarized in the diagram on the following pages. Each of the "nineteenth-century ideologies" listed in the left column refers to ideas which are partially true, but which need to be qualified and criticized in the light of the facts and arguments suggested in the right column. Everyone can think of illustrations of the "twentieth-century realities." Here are some important examples:

- The cost of living has risen alarmingly in recent

[4] Adam Smith, *The Wealth of Nations*, as quoted in George Soule, *Ideas of the Great Economists* (New York: The Viking Press, 1952), pp. 53-54.

[5] Heilbroner, *op. cit.*, pp. 53-55.

years, and inflation has made life increasingly difficult for millions of people on relatively fixed incomes.

• Unemployment is a problem of the utmost seriousness, especially for certain segments of the population, such as blacks, untrained youth, and older persons with obsolescent skills.

• Power in the American economy is getting more and more concentrated each year. Dr. Willard F. Mueller, former chief economist of the Federal Trade Commission, has pointed out: "the top 200 manufacturing corporations already control about 2/3 of all assets held by corporations engaged primarily in manufacturing." After citing Dr. Mueller, Morton Mintz and Jerry Cohen explain:

They have reached this pinnacle primarily through mergers—buying their way to the top.

The sheer magnitude of the merger movement makes it difficult to grasp. In 1968 the one hundred largest corporations had a greater share of manufacturing assets than the two hundred largest had in 1950, and the two hundred largest in 1968 controlled a share equal to that held by the thousand largest in 1941. [6]

THE FREE-MARKET SYSTEM

Nineteenth-Century Ideologies	*Twentieth-Century Realities*
ASSUMPTIONS	
1. *Man is basically an economic being.* He can be counted on to respond to "the cues of the market": he will work, invest, and buy where he can maximize financial gain.	1. Man is (fortunately) much more than an economic being, and he is perfectly capable of putting nonmonetary values (such as Christian love or justice) above financial considerations.
2. *Perfect competition prevails.* Products will keep improving; prices will get lower and lower; and only the best firms will prosper because the market reinforces excellence.	2. Competition does not prevail in a situation where prices can be fixed at an artificially high level, minority group persons can be kept out of certain jobs, new firms or products can be kept out of the market, etc.

[6] Morton Mintz and Jerry S. Cohen, *America, Inc.* (New York: The Dial Press, 1971), p. 35.

Nineteenth-Century Ideologies

3. *Say's Law* decrees that consumption will always equal production, thus making serious depressions and widespread unemployment impossible.

4. *The laws of supply and demand are self-regulating,* and therefore power is not in the hands of men but rather in the impersonal operations of the market.

5. *The proper function of government is limited,* and it must not interfere with the delicate mechanisms of the invisible hand.

Twentieth-Century Realities

3. An economy can be stagnant, and violent cycles of inflation and recession can create unemployment or loss of real wealth for millions of people.

4. Power does rest in the hands of certain individuals and groups, and they must bear responsibility for the consequences of the decisions they make and the influence they wield.

5. The American government has always stepped in to correct the distortions of the market's operations, and if it did not, economic injustice would be even more outrageous than it is.

CLAIMS

a. *Realism about human nature:* the free-market system recognizes man's selfishness and harnesses it.

b. *Efficiency:* by putting a price on things, the free-market system enables people to make decisions easily and insures that work gets done.

c. *Incentive:* creativity, initiative, and hard work are encouraged because they are rewarded.

d. *Freedom:* people can demand what they want by the way they spend, and the market gives them a wide range of choice.

e. *Productivity:* since anything for which a demand exists can be sold, it will get produced, and resources will not lie idle.

CRITICISMS

a. By glorifying selfishness, the ideology of the free-market system makes it worse than it would otherwise be.

b. It is not "efficient" to engulf consumers with a flood of nonessential gadgets when basic goods and services (schools, hospitals, etc.) are inadequate.

c. The incentive is to profit, which can be gained through cutting corners and "figuring an angle," not always through useful work.

d. People can't always buy what they really *want,* only what's offered for sale. And only those with money have genuine choices.

e. Industrial machinery often produces at a level far below capacity, in order to keep supply low and prices and profit high.

TWENTIETH-CENTURY REALITIES

All of the assumptions and claims of the free-market system need to be evaluated in the light of our experience. To acknowledge that fallen man is never able to transcend completely the selfishness that is a part of his sinful nature is one thing. It is quite another to say that the desire for financial gain is his *ruling* motivation and to offer assurances that this desire will somehow work out for the good of everyone. It is one thing to encourage limited competition as a means of stimulating inventiveness and energy, but it is quite another to say that competition must be unrestricted (and its casualties calmly accepted) if its blessings are to be enjoyed. Christian thought has always urged men to love their neighbors and seek their welfare (see especially Matthew 22:36-40), not to do everything possible to outdo or undo them. Some social gospel spokesmen may have been a bit naïve in suggesting that competition was intrinsically unchristian and in proposing that it be replaced entirely by cooperative arrangements in production and distribution. But were they not closer to biblical faith than those who would accept without protest the assumption that man acts only out of economic self-interest.

The greatest limitations on freedom caused by the unrestricted operation of the free-market system in our technological age stem from the "third-party damages" so often inflicted upon innocent bystanders who have no part in transactions which affect them seriously. If a factory has the freedom to pollute a river, the freedom of thousands who live downstream to use that river is curtailed: no more swimming or fishing for them, and maybe higher taxes for their water-supply facilities. If everyone who wants to is free to drive his car into the center of a large city, then everyone who lives there has less freedom to breathe clean air and move about on the city's streets. And if scarce natural resources, such as petroleum, metal ores, and forests, are recklessly depleted by today's producers and consumers, our grandchildren may not be free to enjoy these bounties of creation. [7]

The frequently mentioned "redistribution of wealth," which is supposed to have occurred in this country since the days of the New Deal, has not actually taken place: the top 5 percent of the population still receive 20 percent of the nation's income, and the lowest 20 percent still get only 5 percent of the wealth; furthermore, the highest 20 percent get over 40 percent of the income, whereas the lowest 40 percent get only 16 percent of the wealth. [8] Even the benefits of the division of labor, from which Adam Smith expected so much, are not what they should be, for productivity is held artificially low to boost profits. According to Judge David Bazelon of our nation's capital:

> The main thing to be understood about administered prices is that they are not to be understood at all apart from long-range business planning. That is, a particular price is based on the idea that you are going to sell a particular quantity with given fixed costs and given unit costs. . . . So the main thing price does, in the mind of the price administrator, is to determine how much shall be sold in the first place. For example, it is reported that General Motors uses a "standard volume" system for setting prices. It wants 20 per cent profit after taxes, and figures its price in order to earn this on an "estimated average rate of planned operation." This latter has been calculated on the basis of about 55 per cent of capacity. . . .
>
> U . S . Steel, which must set some 50,000 prices, now has a break-even point of 32 per cent of capacity; the Company could cut its prices 10 per cent and still break even at 50 per cent of capacity, which is the national average. [9]

[7] See Donella H. Meadows, *et al., The Limits to Growth* (New York: Universe Books, 1972).

[8] Herman P. Miller, *Rich Man, Poor Man* (New York: Thomas Y. Crowell Company, 1964), p. 35. Cf. U.S. Bureau of the Census: *Statistical Abstract of the United States: 1971*, 92nd edition (Washington, D.C., 1971), p. 31.

[9] David T. Bazelon, *The Paper Economy* (New York: Random House, Inc., 1963), pp. 210-211.

There is no telling how much prices could be cut, or how many more citizens could enjoy the use of steel products if production took place at the level of 100 percent for several years.

IMPROVING OUR ECONOMIC SYSTEM

Let's face it: the so-called free-market system as it exists in North America today can hardly be called an ideal economic system. True, we can all affirm certain positive values in the system, but our society is constantly changing, and so must our economic system change also. So far it would seem as if most of the changes that have taken place have been in favor of those who have the most. The Christian's goal is to try to guide change in our society so that everyone will have enough. Much of what follows in this chapter may seem to many to be idealistic, but its purpose is to help us see how it may be possible to work through the present system to something which is more just for all.

The seriousness of several impending crises presses upon us the need for a new understanding of what being truly realistic is. In a world where the mass media create a revolution of rising expectations that touches the masses of poor people all over the globe, it is not very realistic to suppose that these hungry millions will continue to accept their grim circumstances as passively as they did in past centuries. The only realistic assessment of their plight and their reaction to it in the future includes recognition that improving their lives is absolutely essential to world peace.[10] The only realistic approach to our environmental crises is to acknowledge that unrestrained plunder or pollution of

[10] See William J. Nottingham, "Youth and Revolution," in Stephen C. Rose, ed., *The Development Apocalypse* (Geneva: World Council of Churches, 1967), pp. 124-130.

the earth's resources *must* be curbed and the standard of living of the overdeveloped nations adjusted accordingly. There is increasingly widespread agreement that the only way the population explosion can be prevented is through the acceptance of what Garrett Hardin aptly calls "mutual coercion, mutually agreed upon." [11]

Given the dangers of undisciplined economic greed and the gravity of a society that allows poverty and poor health to exist, how much longer can we allow so many persons to be deprived without an acceptance of some kind of regulation? Perhaps it is not impossible to model our economic system along the following lines: [12]

1. The purpose of *production* will be to meet human need, not to collect profits, power, pride, or any other consideration that stands in the way of a sensible use of natural resources for the satisfaction of the genuine needs of all members of the commonwealth. *Research* will not be directed toward the development of environmentally destructive or humanly trivial gadgets and gimmicks. It will be directed instead toward conservation of the limited supplies on the spaceship earth and the provision of truly useful and enjoyable supplies for all its inhabitants.

2. In a just economic system, production plants cannot operate below needed capacity in order to insure profits by maintaining prices at an artificially high level. The basic necessities for everyone must be in abundant supply, and everyone should get an adequate share. In some cases this will mean an acceptance of forced sharing of resources through such plans as welfare and free health services.

[11] Garrett Hardin, "The Tragedy of the Commons," *Science*, vol. 162 (Dec. 13, 1968), pp. 1243-1248.

[12] For a fuller exposition of this line of thought, see Henry Clark, *The Irony of American Morality* (New Haven, Conn.: College and University Press, 1971), pp. 215-238.

Christians will need to think in terms of putting the public welfare ahead of private, individual welfare.

3. Work processes will no longer require that the natural rhythms of the human body and the creativity of the human mind and spirit be bent and crushed to suit machines. Much drudgery can be eliminated, and human beings will be free to adopt a variety of life-styles and to choose things they will buy or do.

A BIBLICAL PERSPECTIVE

The fundamental point of view about God's bounty of natural resources and the vocation of an economic system in using them rightly is richly supported by the full range of biblical witnesses. Biblical writers could hardly have imagined a technological society in which economic abundance as we can now enjoy it would be possible. However, all that they had to say about the goodness of creation and the just allocation of its goods to God's people presupposes a reverence for the earth and a sense of concern about and responsibility for the least of the brethren. The Bible does throw light on ways to moderate and reform the economic order of today. The Bible points the way to a sane, humane economy built to meet healthy human needs, not to indulge sinful man's insatiable quest for power.

• The *account of creation* given in Genesis 1 celebrates the wonder and beauty of God's handiwork ("Behold, it was very good!" Genesis 1:31) and entrusts this marvelous gift to the care of mankind. In the Garden of Eden, there was such abundance that greed, exploitation, pride, and anxiety were unnecessary, and generous sharing and free enjoyment could flourish uncontaminated. Technological man will be terribly foolish if he ignores this particular bit of biblical wisdom.

• The *Torah and the historical books* of the Old Testament describe a human community in which the common wealth is always distributed in such a way as to guarantee a decent share of economic goods to even the poorest members of the commonwealth. Gleaning, the custom that allowed poor people to pick up the grain that fell to the ground when the reapers cut the wheat (see Ruth 2), was a *right* of the poor. The prophet Amos uttered furious condemnation on the avaricious landowners who violated this right by "sell[ing] the refuse of the wheat" (Amos 8:6).

Tithing in every third year was used as a means of providing for "the Levite, because he has no portion or inheritance with you, and the sojourner, the fatherless, and the widow" (Deuteronomy 14:28-29). The same kind of mechanism was at work in the institution of the "Year of Jubilee," when debts were to be forgotten and slaves freed (Leviticus 25:8-16, 23-55). Tithing was more than a matter of duty. In certain years it was used for a great feast of thanksgiving and celebration "before the Lord your God, in the place which he will choose, to make his name dwell there." At the thanksgiving ceremony, the Hebrew people were allowed for a time to "spend the money [of the tithe] for whatever you desire . . . whatever your appetite craves" (Deuteronomy 14:23, 26). Biblical faith is wise enough to know that one of the best protections against the cold-blooded acquisitive materialism that causes men to channel their energies into the quest for power and aggrandizement is healthy affirmation of natural feelings and vitalities.

• *The wisdom literature* and the poetry of the Bible are filled with hymns of wonder and celebration that call us away from the frenzied pursuit of pleasures that cannot satisfy and a degree of power that dehumanizes. They urge us to be quieter and more in touch with the mysterious springs of beauty and spiritual power present throughout the creation. Psalm 19 compares the glory of God as declared in the firmament to the exultation of a bridegroom leaving his chamber or that of a strong man experiencing the joy of running. Psalm 23 contains a gentle rebuke to the anxiety about death and competition that so often afflict man. The psalmist reminds the faithful that calmness, abundance, and the reassurance and love symbolized by anointment ought to be the dominant tone of the life of faith. Proverbs 3 declares that wisdom and understanding are more profitable than gold or silver (Proverbs 3:13-14). The kind of wisdom referred to is more than the kind which leads to honesty, generosity, peacefulness.

The following advice is an example of this wisdom:

> Do not contend with a man for no reason,
>> when he has done you no harm.
> Do not envy a man of violence
>> and do not choose any of his ways.
>
> Proverbs 3:30-31

Such wisdom is a *being in tune with the deepest, most mysterious, and most wonderful realities of the universe:* the creative *Logos* of God, reverential awe of whom is the beginning of human wisdom (Proverbs 9:10). How insane is the idolatrous misuse of natural resources in our civilization in comparison with this view of life!

• Everything *the prophets* have to say about fascination with wealth and power, and the unscrupulous behavior to which this fascination leads, is very much to the point here. The gross national product and technological progress are, for all practical purposes, gods to many contemporary Americans. This eloquent passage from Jeremiah is as timely a commentary on our megalomania as anything a contemporary prophet could contrive:

"A tree from the forest is cut down,
  and worked with an axe by the hands
    of a craftsman.
Men deck it with silver and gold;
  they fasten it with hammer and nails
    so that it cannot move.
Their idols are like scarecrows in a cucumber field,
  and they cannot speak;
    they have to be carried,
    for they cannot walk.
Be not afraid of them,
  for they cannot do evil,
    neither is it in them to do good.". . .

They are worthless, a work of delusion;
  at the time of their punishment they shall perish.
Not like these is he who is the portion of Jacob,
  for he is the one who formed all things,
and Israel is the tribe of his inheritance;
  the Lord of hosts is his name.

Jeremiah 10:3-5, 15-16

• The *New Testament* is no more aware of the complexities of modern industrial society or preoccupied with its concerns than the Old Testament. Yet even more than the Old Testament it bespeaks a faith perspective that condemns injustice, hardness of heart, and the kind of materialism that distorts and cripples the human spirit. Jesus' teachings about the lilies of the field (Matthew 6:28-30) and becoming as little children (Matthew 18:1-4) include a rebuke of the folly of our power-mad strivings, our exaggerated anxieties about a type of economic security which is not worth the price, and an inflated notion of comfort that robs us of true joy. In a certain sense, flowers and children are alike in their unhurried, unforced *blossoming*. Unless interfered with by outside forces, they simply take what they need from the surrounding environment, just what they need, no more, and unfold at their own pace, without violating the inner harmony of their being as God has ordained it.

Perhaps even the strange parable about the barren fig tree (Luke 13:6-9) has a startling application not only to Jesus' day but to our own day and age. An economic system which does not produce the fruits that are really needed by the people who depend upon it deserves to be rooted out or modified.

"Lo, these three years I have come seeking fruit on this fig tree, and I find none. Cut it down; why should it use up the ground?" (Luke 13:7). Surely it must be drastically pruned and enriched with a new kind of fertilizer, as the gardener in the parable beseeches: "Let it alone, sir, this year also, till I dig about it and put on manure. And if it bears fruit next year, well and good; but if not, you can cut it down" (Luke 13:8). The promise of another chance is there. But so is the threat of doom if the tree continues to bear no fruit.

4.
Why
the
Poor
Stay
Poor

What does it mean to be poor in America today? Perhaps the best way for you to prepare for your encounter with the material contained in this chapter is to visit one of the poor sections of your town or city. Don't drive, because getting there on foot or by public transportation is an important part of the experience. Stand on a street corner and watch people go by for a while, being sure to take note of their reaction to your unfamiliar presence. Go into a drugstore, a grocery store, or a hamburger joint, and look around, comparing the kinds of commodities on sale and their prices to those you would find in the similar stores you normally patronize. Step into a welfare office, if you can, and see if you can pick up some of the conversation between a welfare mother and the representative of the welfare system with whom she must deal. Find out what the requirements are for acceptance in a public welfare program, or ask what you would have to do to get a job through the state employment agency. As you go back to your own home, try to imagine how you would feel if you had to live in this kind of world for the rest of your life—and how you would feel toward the people who live in the world of at least middle-class comfort.

There are some who say that any concern about poverty based upon our feelings which grow out of such experiences is merely to be "softheaded." Therefore, we must analyze quite carefully just what we mean by poverty in contemporary America.

Who are the poor? There is no such thing as "the poor" in the sense of a vast conglomeration of people who all share exactly the same characteristics and attitudes about their plight. The aged poor are most deeply injured by problems that are secondary for unemployed youth. The female household head wants and needs a different list of benefits than the tenant farmer or the migrant worker. The urban Puerto Rican has complaints that differ significantly from those heard in Appalachia. It is hardly surprising that one of the difficulties faced by social reform strategists is conflict of interest or disagreement about what most urgently needs to be done among different segments of the poor. And these differences make it hard for poor people to unite their efforts in a sophisticated political action campaign for an agreed upon list of common goals.

THE ECONOMIC DIMENSION OF POVERTY

One thing the poor do have in common is their lack of *money*. The economic dimension of poverty is the easiest to define. The usual way of doing this is to choose an annual income figure that can be used as a "poverty line" which separates the poor from the nonpoor. Those who are critical of this approach contend that it is better to think in terms of a "poverty *band*" with an upper and a lower limit, within which a person or a family would be considered poor. Others go even further in their efforts to refine the concept, specifying geographical, age, family size, and other quantitative variables, so that they come up with a poverty line or band for each type of poor person. [1]

The debate is important, because the magnitude of the problem is different according to the level of income selected as the dividing line between poverty and a reasonable standard of living in this society. In 1964, when the dismayingly ineffective "War on Poverty" was being prepared and launched, the Council of Economic Advisers chose the figure of $3,000 for a family of four as a rough indicator of poverty. [2] This figure received wide acceptance for several years in many public discussions of poverty, with proportionate amounts suggested for larger or smaller families.

But these figures were scandalously low. Other government agencies responsible for minimal public standards of nutrition and health were saying that the minimum for a family of four in a large urban center was closer to $5,000. Oscar Ornati, who suggested three different bands ranging from "minimum subsistence" to "minimum adequacy" to "minimum comfort," put the relevant figure in 1960 as high as $5,609 per year. [3] If these figures are used, the extent of poverty in the United States in the mid-sixties

[1] A cogent summary of recent poverty research in the United States is presented in Ben B. Seligman, *Permanent Poverty: An American Syndrome* (Chicago: Quadrangle Books, 1968), pp. 21-39.

[2] Herman P. Miller, *Rich Man, Poor Man* (New York: Thomas Y. Crowell Company, 1964), pp. 56-83.

[3] Oscar Ornati, *Poverty Amid Affluence* (New York: Twentieth Century Fund, Inc., 1966).

was not Miller's 18 percent; it was more like the 40 percent estimate made by Leon Keyserling.[4] That estimate would mean more than 80 million persons living in poverty or deprivation! And that's 30 million more than Michael Harrington's estimate of 50 million in 1963.[5]

In a society as rich as ours, it is surely the higher estimates which ought to be used. (Up-to-date figures would have to be considerably higher in dollar terms to represent the same buying power in today's currency.) The hidden assumptions must be examined: What is "minimum" subsistence or minimum "adequacy"? Does a man *require* a certain type of diet or housing or a certain level of medical and dental care to survive?

Probably not. Even if his body is stunted and his intelligence *permanently retarded* because of malnutrition,[6] and even if he suffers constant agony of body and spirit because of his untreated diseases, discomforts, and anxieties, man can remain alive for quite a long time. But let us rejoice that one of the signs of God's grace, one of the manifestations of his image in man in the modern world, is the horror most people feel at the thought of simply "letting it go at that." We cannot bear to think of human beings "living like animals," as we say. Humanity is more than survival. Any honest definition of poverty must deal with psychological and philosophical dimensions of it as well as its strictly economic dimensions. *Welfare* needs and *fulfillment* needs as well as *survival* needs must be taken into consideration.

[4] Leon Keyserling, *Poverty and Deprivation in the United States* (Washington, D.C.: Conference on Economic Progress, 1962).

[5] Michael Harrington, *The Other America* (New York: The Macmillan Company, 1962), pp. 1-18.

[6] Rodger L. Hurley, *Poverty and Mental Retardation: A Causal Relationship* (New York: Random House, Inc., 1969).

THE PSYCHO-CULTURAL DIMENSION OF POVERTY

The psycho-cultural aspects of poverty have to be analyzed because of the fact that definitions of the quality of *human* life change in time and across cultural boundaries. Man is not a biological atom. He is always a *self-in-community* whose being is defined in relation to his society and its standards. Time and technological change make former fulfillment needs into welfare needs, and earlier welfare needs into survival needs. A certain degree of involuntary deprivation of worldly goods that are considered necessary in a given society *de-grades* a person. Such deprivation disqualifies him from the "grade" (the rank, the status, the position) essential to human identity in that society.[7] This kind of cruelty can be tolerated only if it is absolutely unavoidable. Since in our society it *can* be avoided, shouldn't a Christian affirm that it *ought* to be?

If the soundness of this line of reasoning is granted, then in a technologically advanced society in which affluence is a possibility for all, to deprive a citizen of those things commonly regarded as necessities is an affront to human dignity. Other implications of this line of argument which might be mentioned are:

• Given the conditions of an age of scarcity, in which the tribe desperately needed some contribution of labor from every member in order to insure bare survival in the face of natural conditions which they could neither understand nor control, there were some legitimate grounds for saying that those who did not work should not eat. Given an age of abundance in which the labor of everyone is not required, should this demand be made upon such

[7] John Kenneth Galbraith, *The Affluent Society* (Boston: Houghton Mifflin Company, 1958), pp. 323-324.

persons as the aged, the infirm, children, mothers of small children, or creative artists?

• Given a culture in which the unemployed are severely stigmatized, does society have an obligation either to provide work for those who feel that their humanity requires it, or to undertake an educational campaign which will release them from bondage to an attitude toward work which has become obsolete?

• Given a society in which excellent medical care is possible, is equal access to its benefits a legitimate right of everyone? If an increase in the supply of doctors and health workers is necessary to satisfy the demand, should society provide for that increase, regardless of the objections of professional medical associations?

• Given a society in which the aged had a place of dignity within extended families encompassing several generations, there was no need for special measures to integrate older people into the full life of the community. With the decline of the extended family, the prolongation of life, and the idolatry of youthfulness characteristic of our culture, are more extraordinary measures perhaps necessary to make a place in our lives for senior citizens?

• Given a situation in which one is demonstrably out of touch with the pulse of life without a number of commodities or experiences deemed virtual necessities by a majority of people in our society, should we call such possessions and opportunities "luxuries"? Could they be necessary to welfare, if not actually needed for survival? Could the deprival of these options constitute a restriction on the freedom and humanity of the persons concerned? Poverty has a spiritual value only if it is freely chosen.

Voluntarily chosen poverty is accepted as a spiritual discipline by individuals who want to free their souls from the complications engendered by life in the world. Some persons have the marvelous capacity of grace to transmute suffering into inner growth. But not everyone is given the grace required to grow spiritually through the disciplines of poverty, and certainly not everyone should be expected to attempt this path in life. For all practical purposes, it is tragic when children cannot develop physiologically, mentally, and emotionally because of poverty. Poverty should not be forced upon anyone who prefers to live as a participating member in modern society.

What can we say then about this portrait of poverty which includes psychological and cultural dimensions as well as an economic dimension? Most would agree that the economic aspects of poverty should be mitigated as far as possible, consistent with the need to leave room for the operation of individual initiative and free choice. Much more difficult questions arise in regard to the psychocultural dimensions of poverty. Perhaps the most grievous psychological sting associated with being poor in America is the societal and interpersonal isolation—the degradation—one is apt to feel. In less affluent societies, the poor are a majority; or, if they are not, they are seldom made to feel as excluded and displaced as they are in twentieth-century America. In ancient Israel, for example, gleaning was a solidly established *right*, and gleaners toiled in the fields right along with the threshers. (See Ruth 2 and Leviticus 19:9-10.) A person in our society who exists by raiding garbage cans is in for much more miserable treatment. If we can analyze our feelings about such a person, we will begin to comprehend the psychological dimensions of poverty.

A BIBLICAL PERSPECTIVE

Much of the hardhearted talk about poverty one hears

among relatively comfortable people today is covered over with a gloss of ignorant sentimentality which fails to take into account the painfulness and the dehumanizing impact of economic deprivation.

One frequently hears the expression "the poor are always with us," alluding to the passage in Mark 14:3-9. Jesus was merely saying that Mary's act of personal devotion to him on the eve of his crucifixion was at that moment more valuable and more sincerely motivated than Judas's highly questionable concern for the poor. The Gospels are full of rebukes to the rich (see Matthew 6:25; Mark 10:17-22; Matthew 19:24) and hardly sentimental about the spiritual consequences of dire poverty.

The prophets knew that poverty often drives men to do unspeakably horrifying things, such as selling a son into slavery or a daughter into prostitution. That's what Amos's denunciation of those who "buy the poor for silver and the needy for a pair of sandals" refers to in Amos 8:6. The bribery, the strikebreaking, and many other kinds of extortion that men of wealth and power depend upon to maintain their control over things could not exist without the desperate circumstances of the poor.

WHY DO THE POOR STAY POOR?

Many readers of this book have no difficulty in recognizing the hardships of being poor. They may have been poor in their own childhood. They may still consider themselves so hard-pressed as to be always on the verge of poverty. What is more difficult to understand is the apparent satisfaction of some poor people who don't seem to be making much effort to rise above their condition, or to make it as dignified as possible.

There are three possible answers to this puzzle:

1. *The "culture of poverty" or "the vicious circle of poverty."* From the standpoint of mainstream American culture, many of the traits often associated with poverty are shortcomings which deserve to be criticized. But many of these very traits continue to exist because they "make sense" in the total life situation of many poor people and are very helpful in the life they are forced to lead. Lack of thrift, for example, is largely the result of the fact that in their experience thrift doesn't pay. The wad of money stuffed into a mattress is stolen. If we ask why they didn't take the money to a bank, we fail to realize that many poor people do not understand, trust, or feel at home in institutions like banks.

Some poor people feel that it is pointless to look in the newspaper for employment opportunities outside the neighborhood. That world beyond the boundaries of the familiar is strange and hostile. Those who venture into it often come to no good end—or they don't come back at all.

Many poor people exist in a subcultural atmosphere where their greatest strength and comfort is a consciousness of kind that insulates them from the outside world and its standards. It leads them to elaborate special norms and limited expectations appropriate to what middle-class America tells them is their inferior status.

2. *Pluralism of American culture.* Occasionally the alienation implied in the concept of a culture of poverty becomes self-conscious and hostile. In cases where this is true, the result is a militant separatism which demands self-determination and rejects conformity to mainstream values and norms as a loss of integrity that cannot be countenanced. In a job-training program in Oakland, California, this kind of separatist mentality led to refusal on the part of young black men to cultivate certain standard American behavioral characteristics which most employers would feel justified in

requiring: punctuality, beardless faces, no dark glasses while on the job, and standard English in on-the-job conversation. [8] Similar conflicts between the expectations of employers and the sense of identity of potential employees raise extremely difficult questions about justice and cultural pluralism in a democratic society. Is there a need for a revised definition of prevailing notions about the shortcomings of the poor? How much should the poor be expected to conform to mainstream behavior patterns?

3. *Pressure from above.* The crucial cause of economic injustice in our country today is neither the utility of different social practices in the culture of poverty nor the self-conscious preference for a different style of life by people who don't want to be standard-brand Americans in all respects. The root cause of discrimination against the "have nots" and the bias in favor of the "haves" which are deeply rooted in the American economic and political system is what the next chapter is all about.

[8] See David Wellman, "The *Wrong* Way to Find Jobs for Negroes," *Trans-action*, vol. 5 (April, 1968), pp. 9-18.

5.
How
the
Rich
Stay
Rich

Very few people are ever entirely out of debt, and nobody who cares about keeping his bills paid is ever free of economic worries. But think for a moment about the degree of security you probably do enjoy:

• Do you own your own home? If so, it is probably held on a not-yet-fully-paid mortgage. The interest you pay on that mortgage loan is tax-deductible. Perhaps you got a mortgage at lower interest rates because of a government-supported program for home loans. In fact, you may have been able to get a mortgage loan only because the loan was covered by government insurance. Doesn't this represent a sizable subsidy?

• Many of the appliances and pieces of furniture in your home may have been purchased on installment-payment plans or through credit arrangements which you had little difficulty in obtaining. You entered into those arrangements without having any anxiety about the honesty of your creditors. Do you think that you could probably get credit again any time you need to ?

• Do you have insurance policies on your home and its contents? Probably it has not occurred to you that a person in your position could have any serious difficulty obtaining as much insurance as you like.

• Do you have a Social Security card in your wallet? If so, you are relieved of considerable anxiety as you think of retirement. You know you will be protected by Medicare in your old age, and that any medical treatment needed by your elderly parents will not have to be paid for entirely out of their savings or yours.

• If you own a car, the thought of it may remind you of the nice trips you have taken or those you may be planning to take in the future on America's superb highway system.

• What about the neighborhood in which you live? Does it provide you with excellent schools, well-paved and comfortably lighted streets, adequate police and fire protection, and many other reliable public services?

If you can count most of the above items in your list of economic blessings, you are very lucky. You should not take these blessings for granted; indeed, you should be more humbly aware that you are the favored beneficiary of a political, economic, and social system which is heavily biased in favor of some citizens at the expense of others. Every one of the securities noted above is the manifestation of some government program or priority that bestows more benefits on those who already have a relative sufficiency instead of meeting more basic and pressing needs of the poor. What we have in this country is actually "socialism for the rich and free enterprise for the poor," because the poorest segments of the population have not benefited as much from the many programs of social welfare legislation of the past fifty years as have those with slightly higher incomes.

If you have difficulty in understanding why the poor resent some of these benefits which many tend to think are well deserved, think for a moment about your reaction to the huge salaries received by movie stars, entertainers, and sports heroes. Most of us would probably say that such people don't really deserve to make that much more money than hard-working people. In like fashion, many lower-income people have great difficulty in rationalizing and accepting the reasons that middle-class people give to explain why their incomes and other benefits are so large in comparison to what the poor receive.

We need to explore the contention that the root cause of the deprivation of the poor in America is the oppressive exercise of power in the form of laws, procedures, and customs that systematically keep the poor at a disadvantage. Attitudes and institutions—powerful attitudes and institutions—keep the poor poor and enable the rich to stay rich.

One of the most deplorable attitudes that perpetuates poverty is the hardness of heart toward the poor which accompanies the always rigorous and sometimes harsh self-discipline of the affluent person. He has made it the hard way himself, and he thinks that everyone else ought to have to make it the same way. This attitude leads to the kind of resentment portrayed by the older brother in the parable of the prodigal son. (See Luke 15:25-30.)

Some middle-class people fear that equal opportunity for the dispossessed may mean more competition for them and for their children. Thus, many middle-class taxpayers are less than enthusiastic about paying higher taxes so that slum dwellers may have better schools, unemployed men may have retraining, and dependent children may have adequate provision for food and clothing. Those who have managed to build a little security and comfort for themselves by their own hard work tend to be resentful of special opportunities, which they never enjoyed, being offered to others.

But these attitudinal evils form only the tip of the iceberg. The crucial and much larger part of the problem is formed by the institutionalized injustices which are so much a part of the system, of *everyday life,* that we hardly notice them. These injustices may best be understood under four principal headings: sins of commission, sins of omission, hidden subsidies, and regressive public welfare policies.

SINS OF COMMISSION

The most obvious point of departure for a discussion of the abuses of power which reinforce poverty is a catalog of some of the most important ways in which consumers are manipulated, defrauded, and even coerced by the selling and lending firms with which they have dealings, and of the ways in which millions of workers are victimized by low pay or dehumanizing working conditions.

An economic system that increases the winnings of the victors in direct proportion to the losses inflicted upon the vanquished, and which measures victory primarily in monetary terms, is bound to encourage a spirit of competition so aggressive as to become quite often exploitative. Four examples can be cited here to illustrate the point:

1. *Planned obsolescence.* If your car is "a lemon," your new washing machine breaks down within a year, and your clothes go out of style before you ever have them dry cleaned,

it may not be an accident. It may be at least in part the result of careful planning on the part of manufacturers whose profits depend upon your buying replacements promptly and repeatedly.[1]

2. *Installment buying and loans.* Many installment buying plans and lending agencies are legal, if not exactly what the medieval moralists who condemned usury would have called ethical. But many, especially those which concentrate on the poor, are not. This unsavory situation has been brought to light recently in many newspaper and magazine articles. Hillel Black's *Buy Now, Pay Later* tells a peculiarly heartrending story about a Puerto Rican worker in Chicago who was actually driven to commit suicide because of the harassments, humiliations, threats, and losses, including garnishment of his wages and, finally, possible loss of his job, perpetrated upon him by unscrupulous merchants who enrich themselves by preying upon the relatively unsuspecting and helpless poor of the city.[2]

3. *Shoddy workmanship.* Almost everyone has been inconvenienced or even endangered at one time or another by the carelessness or laziness of someone who didn't do what he contracted to do. But do we really appreciate the far-reaching implications of the decline of reliable service? Some observers contend that a very high proportion of the disillusionment of American youth in recent years is the consequence of their disgust with the lack of honesty and pride of workmanship characteristic of some of the adults with whom they come into contact, including executives,

[1] The shocking details regarding planned obsolescence in America are presented in Vance Packard, *The Waste Makers* (New York: David McKay Co., Inc., 1960).

[2] Hillel Black, *Buy Now, Pay Later* (New York: William Morrow and Company, 1961), pp. 124-127.

teachers, stenographers, and clerks as well as mechanics, salesmen, and assembly-line personnel.[3]

4. *Exploitation of workers.* A very prominent fact of life for millions of Americans in the labor force is that workers are exploited even though labor unions are strong in some parts of the country. Thousands of American workers are neither protected by the bargaining power of unions nor covered by the social welfare legislation that is supposed to establish a decent economic floor under the feet of all employees through minimum wage, unemployment insurance, and social security. Laundry employees, sanitation workers, household servants, hospital employees, migrant laborers, and even textile-mill personnel are among the employed but severely underpaid members of the labor force who make up a substantial portion of the 20 percent of our population that is poor, and a large portion of the additional 20 percent which must be classified as deprived. [4]

SINS OF OMISSION

The cardinal evil of our economic system today is its *favoritism toward the affluent.* Too many persons know how to get lucrative contracts, fill out their tax returns, apply for research grants, and, in short, play the business game as the current laws allow it to be played.

On the other hand, poor people do not actually have equal protection under the law. They are more likely to be arrested and less able to get out on bail pending trial. Because they can't afford a good attorney, they are more likely to be convicted; because they can't pay a fine, they are more likely

[3] Paul Goodman, *Growing Up Absurd* (New York: Random House, 1956), pp.17-30.

[4] For a study of this subject see Leon H. Keyserling, *The Role of Wages in a Great Society: Stressing Minimum-Wage Gains to Help the Working Poor* (Washington, D.C.: Conference on Economic Progress, 1966).

to be sent to jail if convicted, and much more likely to be dragged down into a life of crime because of a first, sometimes minor, offense. They are frequently unable to secure fair treatment in welfare programs or other kinds of bureaucratic arrangements. They are at the mercy of clerks and administrators whose interpretation of administrative policies and regulations they seldom feel able to contest. The poor are desperately in need of legal aid services and official "watchdogs" to help insure fair treatment under existing laws.

The political aspect of the double standard favoring the affluent is manifested in a host of escape hatches. These enable the shrewd and powerful to avoid prosecution for legal violations that cause far more damage to far more people than the relatively personal and petty acts committed by poor criminals. For example, originally bankruptcy laws were intended as protective devices to prevent poverty. Today these laws are being abused in many cases. In *The Paper Economy,* David Bazelon explains how clever manipulators can even arrange their dealings so as to make sizable profits out of a bankruptcy.[5]

Some stock-market operators swindle hundreds of helpless investors and may never be prosecuted for their crimes. Some executives of large corporations whose price-fixing collusion robs taxpayers of millions of dollars either avoid indictment altogether or get off with extremely light sentences.[6] Weak and poorly enforced antitrust laws sometimes constitute another kind of legal immunity enjoyed by the rich and the powerful.

[5] David Bazelon, *The Paper Economy* (New York: Random House, Inc., 1963), pp. 112-115.

[6] Richard Ney, *The Wall Street Jungle* (New York: Grove Press, Inc., 1970), pp. 111-125; John Herling, *The Great Price Conspiracy* (Washington, D.C.; Robert B. Luce, Inc., 1962).

HIDDEN SUBSIDIES

More pervasive, however, and infinitely more harmful in their consequences for millions of citizens, are the subsidies that are given to those who already have quite a lot. The very word calls to mind direct payments made by the government to farmers whose idle land enriches them, or tax credits, such as the 22 percent oil depletion allowance that adds to the profits of the petroleum industry. The most significant subsidies are those which are often hidden and indirect. These are the huge payoffs that accrue from "normal business operations" or from government programs ostensibly undertaken for some other objective.

By far the most lucrative of these hidden subsidies are the government contracts typical of Department of Defense procurement practices which have led to the incredible profit-pyramiding unearthed by congressional investigations in recent years. The purchase of equipment is not the only type of contract that contributes to the profits of those who do business with the government. Research contracts can also give a lucky firm a tremendous windfall in the form of government-financed development of new products or processes. Even apparently worthwhile social services offer opportunities for excessive profits. The rent-subsidy program was accepted more for its benefits for real estate, banking, and construction interests than for the help it offered to the poor.

Everyone is familiar with the tax loopholes which allow wealthy men and powerful businesses to pay only a fraction of the sum one would expect them to pay if their real income were matched against the official tax tables. Most tax reforms to date have not closed most of these tax loopholes.

Even government efforts to curb inflation often benefit the

rich more than the poor, and may even create more of a problem for the poor. If policies are designed to limit the expansion of production, greater unemployment may follow. While the profits of corporations suffer, the marginal employee who is laid off and cannot find another job is hurt much more crucially. Such a person indeed may have a very difficult time if public spending on social welfare is cut at the same time.

REGRESSIVE PUBLIC WELFARE PROGRAMS

Public welfare measures which seem on the surface to be an example of society's effort to help its poor are often regressive in much the same way that a sales tax is. As Harold Wilensky and Charles Lebeaux observe in their superb study, *Industrial Society and Social Welfare,* there is an ironic discrepancy between modern affirmations of the idea of a limited welfare state and the actual regressiveness and general inadequacy of existing welfare laws and administrative practices. The fact is that "welfare programs have had [only] a small income-equalizing effect within the lower strata and a still smaller effect on the income distribution as a whole."[7] There are three principal reasons for this:

1. The largest, most accepted, and therefore secure, fastest-growing welfare programs—those which are in some sense "social insurance"—are the least egalitarian:

> The main effect of social insurance programs is not a shift of income from rich to poor but from average families to families at the bottom; most of the redistribution occurs within the population having annual family incomes below $5,000 or $6,000.

[7] Harold L. Wilensky and Charles N. Lebeaux, *Industrial Society and Social Welfare* (New York: The Free Press, 1965), p. 159. The discussion which follows is drawn from pp. xiii-xvi.

And the converse is equally true. The most egalitarian programs—those drawn from general federal revenues as opposed to pay-as-you-go or pay-for-future-use programs—are the ones we continue to starve.

2. The benefits paid in some welfare programs, like Medicare, for example, actually represent a flow of funds from the public purse to pay for something which many well-off persons, or their children, could have taken care of themselves from their own private funds. So the already well-to-do may be rewarded, even though unconsciously.

3. The *size* of benefit payments is still miserly. The weekly benefit for an unemployed person who happens to be one of the lucky 25 percent of the labor force covered by such insurance is, on the average, only around $36. He may be entitled to receive this amount only twelve weeks or so. The average payment for a dependent child in a fatherless family of three is only about $23 per week.

To compound the problem, states often use their administrative powers under the federal system to oppress minorities. They can even enforce virtual slavery on the utterly dependent person who can be forced to do some menial work at the alternative of jail or removal from the welfare list.

THE PROPHETIC PROTEST AGAINST OPPRESSION

The Christian who turns to the Bible to find help in understanding the will of God concerning economic justice in our day and time is immediately struck by the remarkable *specificity* of the stirring pronouncements of the Old Testament prophets on these matters.

It is easy to see what and whom the spokesmen of the Lord were condemning in passages which denounced those who "covet fields, and seize them" and "oppress a man and his house" (Micah 2:2), or "those who fill their master's house with violence and fraud" (Zephaniah 1:9). Dishonesty was assailed in very specific terms by Micah, who spoke of "treasures of wickedness in the house of the wicked," "the scant measure that is accursed," "wicked scales," and "a bag of deceitful weights" (Micah 6:10-11). Isaiah referred to avaricious men who "have devoured the vineyard" and are guilty of "grinding the face of the poor" in order to have "the spoil of the poor" in their houses (Isaiah 3:14-15). Jeremiah likened men of unjust wealth to hunters pursuing game:

> For wicked men are found among my people;
>   they lurk like fowlers lying in wait.
> They set a trap;
>   they catch men.
> Like a basket full of birds,
>   their houses are full of treachery;
> therefore they have become great and rich,
>   they have grown fat and sleek.
> They know no bounds in deeds of wickedness;
>   they judge not with justice
> the cause of the fatherless, to make it prosper,
>   and they do not defend the rights of the needy.
>
>   Jeremiah 5:26-28

Consider, too, the condemnation heaped upon government officials in such passages as:

> "I will punish the officials and the king's sons
>   and all who array themselves in foreign attire."
>   Zephaniah 1:8

> So the law is slacked
>   and justice never goes forth.
> For the wicked surround the righteous,
>   so justice goes forth perverted.
>   Habakkuk 1:4

> Her officials within her
>   are roaring lions;
> her judges are evening wolves
>   that leave nothing till the morning.
>
> Zephaniah 3:3

> The prince and the judge ask for a bribe,
> and the great man utters the evil desire of his soul.
>
> Micah 7:3

In Micah 3:1-4 "the rulers of the house of Israel" were accused, figuratively speaking, of cannibalism, and in verses 9 and 10 the prophet condemned public officials who "give judgment for a bribe," priests who "teach for hire," and prophets who "divine for money." Hireling intellectuals and clergymen have always been available to create and peddle whatever ideology the ruling classes want to have as a smokescreen for their evil doings. Micaiah ben Imlah (1 Kings 22) and Amos (Amos 7:10-12) had to contend with court priests and false prophets who specialized in telling the king just exactly what he wanted to hear, and who warned the true prophets to "Go, flee away to the land of Judah, and eat bread there, and prophesy there; but never again prophesy at Bethel, for it is the king's sanctuary, and it is the temple of the kingdom."

The "taunt songs" of Habakkuk 2 warn against debauchery, pride, and greed; and the book of Revelation contains similar warnings against the "merchants of the earth . . . grown rich with the wealth of . . . wantonness" (Revelation 18:3).

But the most important attacks upon misuse of power vis-a-vis the poor are found in Jesus' denunciation of the hypocritical self-righteousness of the Pharisees, who "tithe mint and dill and cummin, and have neglected the weightier matters of the law, justice and mercy and faith" and are "full of extortion and rapacity" (Matthew 23:23,25). If one applies a bit of plausible imagination to the spirit of the Sermon on the Mount (especially the injunctions in Matthew 5:40-41 to "go the second mile" and "give your cloak also"), is it at all farfetched to imagine Jesus continuing his teachings about new law along the following lines?

You have heard that it hath been said of old,
"Thou shalt not be dishonest in business dealings."
But I say unto you, anyone who is scrupulously honest about financial details within an economic system that robs and destroys human beings on a worldwide scale is guilty of thievery and murder.

You have heard that it hath been said of old,
"Thou shalt honor the civil law, for without it civilized order is impossible in human society."
But I say unto you, anyone who merely observes existing laws complacently, without making an effort to change those laws and administrative practices which contribute to the oppression of the poor, is guilty of the evil that is pressed upon them and of the violence and hatred engendered by their oppression.

You have heard that it hath been said of old,
"Thou shalt charge only a just price and pay a fair wage."
But I say unto you, anyone who does not give at least as much attention to the genuine human value of what he develops through research and then markets, and to the instincts he appeals to in his advertising, as he does to the justice of his profit margin is partly responsible for the insanity and the iniquity of "consumerism." And anyone who does not give at least as much support to fully institutionalized programs for income maintenance for the unemployed and the unemployable as he does to fair wages is partly responsible for their misery.

When Judas had led the Roman soldiers to Jesus in the Garden of Gethsemane, our Lord looked upon him sorrowfully and said, "Would you betray the Son of man with a kiss?" (Luke 22:48). Could it be that to us present-day church members Jesus might well say, "Would you betray me with the kind of minimal worship and virtue which pose no real threat to your enjoyment of the fruits of your participation in an often evil and unjust economic system?"

6.
Poverty
and Injustice
in the
Underdeveloped
Countries

Thus far we have considered only the problems of the poor in America. But can we face up to our own materialism adequately without standing face-to-face with the poor of two-thirds of the world? Their misery is probably beyond anything you have ever seen or imagined possible. There is an enormous gap between the comfort of our lives and the wretchedness of theirs. We would consider it intolerable to live for one day the way they have to live practically every day of their lives.

If you want to try to understand what life is like in the underdeveloped nations, you must do the following things: [1]

---

[1] The idea for this startling demonstration of life in an underdeveloped country comes from Robert L. Heilbroner, "The Tableau of Underdevelopment," in Arthur I. Blaustein and Roger R. Woock, eds., *Man Against Poverty: World War III* (New York: Random House, Inc., 1968), pp. 274-277.

—Move all furniture and appliances out of the smallest, most dimly lit room in your house. You may bring in a couple of throw rugs or a piece of canvas to sit on in the daytime and to sleep on at night.

—Turn off the heat or the air-conditioning, and take the screen off the window if you have it open. Your only source of illumination after dark is a candle, and you can allow yourself one blanket for each two adults and one for every three children.

—Needless to say, there is no electricity; so you can forget the radio, the phonograph, the TV, etc. You wouldn't have a newspaper or any books, either; in fact, you wouldn't miss them, because you wouldn't know how to read anyhow. Bring in the charcoal grill and build a wood fire in it for cooking, but the wood must be gathered by hand from the yard, the roadside, or garbage cans.

—Your menu? A saucer of rice, beans, or potatoes is all you get, with maybe a quarter loaf of bread and as much water as you feel like fetching in a pan from your neighbor's (to simulate going to the well or the public fountain).

—Unless you have a yard big enough and private enough to use it as a toilet, there is no way for you to imitate this aspect of life in the underdeveloped countries. Just use your imagination on this one.

—If you go anywhere, go on foot, and don't buy anything all day. Don't use the telephone. In fact, you can add realistic fatigue to your image of the day by trying to do eight hours of hard work on that diet and see how you feel by sundown.

Too much trouble? Unnecessary? Maybe. But surely our thinking so and our reluctance really to carry out such an experiment are some of the best indications imaginable of the enormous gap between the comfort of our lives and the wretchedness of theirs.

While we can, perhaps, begin to imagine what life must be like in the poorer two-thirds of the world, we also probably have a number of questions about this poverty. Why does it continue when we have been pouring in millions of dollars of relief, loans, and investment funds for over twenty-five years? Why can't the people of these countries make any progress in their efforts at economic development? While we have aided them and they are making some progress, we also need to ask just who in these countries is benefiting? Can the rate of progress keep up with the rate of growth? In order to find the answers to these questions and others like them, we need to look again at the situation.

ECONOMIC IMPERIALISM

The picture which shapes up as we look at the underdeveloped countries is one that is best described in the term "economic imperialism." This term does not mean that America is deliberately malevolent or consciously exploitative. It just means that the international trade system and the international political situation call for policies that actually *increase* the economic gap between the rich nations and the poor ones. As Michael Harrington observes:

> Everyone knows that it is more profitable to invest in safe projects than in risky ones—in European and American affluence rather than in Third World poverty. Given the political and social outlook of private business, available funds will go to private rather than to public enterprises, and to undertakings in the ex-colonies only when they promote a quick profit rather than balanced growth of the whole society. *The priorities so skillfully built into the very structure of the international economy are often a more efficient, and subtle, way of keeping the world's poor in their unhappy place than were the gunboats and troops of the earlier imperialism.* To do incalculable harm to the masses of the Third World, the Western politician or businessman need not be evil, but only reasonable and realistic. [2]

[2] Michael Harrington, "American Power in the Twentieth Century," in Arthur I. Blaustein and Roger R. Woock, *op. cit.*, p. 18. Reprinted from *Dissent* Magazine.

The charge is far too complex to be fully explained here, but the outline of an explanation would include the following major points:

1. Our trade with the Third World is no longer as crudely exploitative as it was in the colonial era. Then European and American business firms simply extracted the raw materials and agricultural produce of the underdeveloped countries at prices and under conditions which were often unfair and even dishonest. But it is still true that we tend to milk their industry and plantations for what we need without giving the nationals a fair share of the bounty represented in the resources of their own country. Furthermore, the international market puts them at the mercy of fluctuating demand in the rich nations and forces them to accept the prices we offer at a given time. [3]

2. The kind of industrialization being wrought in the "have not" nations with the benefit of loans and investment funds from the "have" powers gives priority to our desires to make our lives even more prosperous and comfortable instead of to their needs to overcome dire poverty. It makes them dependent on us and keeps them from developing the types of industry they most need to produce what their people most need. Government loans from America, for example, usually help to finance the building of such things as roads, port facilities, and airports, instead of decent housing, irrigation facilities, and hospitals.

In much the same way, private investment funds from the rich nations do not go for high-priority survival and welfare needs of the impoverished majority in the emerging nation,

[3] James Becket, "The World Economy: Short on Change," in Stephen C. Rose, ed., *The Development Apocalypse* (Geneva: World Council of Churches, 1967), pp. 11-29.

because there would be little profit in that. These funds build factories to produce the low-utility glamour items—soft drinks, automobiles, cosmetics—which a small but growing middle class can be trained to want by the importation of magazines and other channels of advertising from Europe and America. That's why the downtown areas of major cities in the Third World look much like ours. But on the outskirts, and out in the countryside, misery is growing worse and worse.

3. This pattern of "dependent industrialization" creates in a Third-World nation the kind of citizen who has more of a *vested interest in foreign patrons* and employers than in the welfare of his own people. Citizens of this kind are not likely to tax themselves more heavily or undertake other costly steps to alleviate the poverty of their less fortunate countrymen. They are tasting some of the pleasures of urban "consumerism." They will want more and more of these exciting new pleasures before they are satisfied enough to turn their attention to the needs of the poor in their own country.

4. Finally, *legal and political leverage* by the rich nations is always present to insure the effective force of economic incentives and psychological inertia. Partial ownership and marginal administrative control are often put into the hands of nationals, but ultimate control and the lion's share of the profits remain in the hands of foreign firms. Parent corporations in the developed nations are able to draw upon accumulated capital in order to finance new plants and equipment, thus achieving economies in the use of venture capital that are not available to the struggling new companies in developing nations. Also, the large corporations, whether based in one country or multi-national, are able to practice economies of scale that a local

firm cannot match. Consequently, large corporations in the developed nations are in a position to freeze out competition and to achieve a monopoly position by buying out any local company whose facilities and established markets they want.

An additional complication is that in recent years the financial assistance extended to these Third-World nations by America has been largely for paramilitary operations and police-related enterprises.

THE NEED FOR PLURALISM

If the current pattern is so unjust, what alternatives exist? What path of economic development can and ought to be followed by the Third World, and what changes in our thinking and the policies of our government would be involved? What is our Christian responsibility for the underdeveloped countries?

The most basic answer to all these questions is this: The best pattern of development will be different for each country, and *the most helpful thing the rich nations can do is not impose their cultural, economic, or political patterns and needs on the poor nations.*

The first step is to get over the idea that everything American or Western is by definition *better.* The technology, the organizational characteristics, and the patterns of consumption and leisure typical of each culture are somewhat different. Many persons deplore the bringing of many of the so-called labor-saving devices of our modern world into the Third-World nations because of the cultural shock which they occasion.

Ivan D. Illich in his book *Celebration of Awareness* contends that the importation of trucks does as much damage in some Third-World countries as the importation of military weapons designed to prevent revolutionary activity. The trucks are too few in number, too expensive in price, and too dependent upon equally scarce and expensive spare parts to be really useful to most of the people. However, once they have seen the trucks, they are no longer willing to work with burros and the simpler lifting and hauling devices which they can build and repair with the materials, the tools, and the knowledge which they have on hand in plentiful supply.[4]

Robert D. Heilbroner, speaking from his perspective as an economic historian, is also skeptical of the possibility of the kind of "technological leap" which would enable a developing nation to go straight from a relatively primitive economy to the post-industrial era. He argues that:

> . . . it is impossible to proceed to the age of the steam-mill until one has passed through the age of the hand-mill, and . . . one cannot move to the age of the hydroelectric plant before one has mastered the steam-mill, not to the nuclear power age until one has lived through that of electricity.[5]

If these authorities are correct in their views, cultural imperialism on the part of the dominant nations may be just as damaging as economic imperialism. This is particularly true when the two are joined together in an assault which tries to create new markets for the foreign-controlled industries by advertisements, mass-media programming, and changes in the educational system that shatter an existing culture and divide its people into a client-middle class, who are satisfied as well as used, and the peons whose interests are not served at all.

Three characteristics of rapid economic development raise particularly difficult questions for us. These are: (1) the corruption in the administration of aid or other

---

[4] Ivan D. Illich, *Celebration of Awareness* (Garden City, N.Y.: Doubleday & Company, Inc., Anchor Books, 1971), pp. 157-174.

[5] Robert L. Heilbroner, *Between Capitalism and Socialism* (New York: Random House, Inc., Vintage Books, 1970), pp. 149-150.

development funds; (2) the necessity for a "one-party democracy" in many countries with a history of severe tribal conflict; and (3) the existence of strong centralized governments which for all practical purposes force an unwilling populace to do what has to be done to overcome poverty. Yet some authorities regard these problems as virtually inevitable in an economically emerging nation.

A certain amount of corruption and waste seems almost inevitable in a time of rapid development. One only has to recall the experience of the United States in the nineteenth century when the railroads and factories were being built and large corporations were being formed to meet the needs of the rapidly growing nation. This is not to excuse corruption, but merely to recognize it as one of the costs of rapid development.

The very term "one-party democracy" strikes the American ear as a contradiction in terms, and perhaps it is. But those who argue its necessity are simply trying to point out that the needs of a fledgling nation's people cannot possibly be served if the animosities which so long have separated its constituent parts are not submerged long enough for some one leadership element to establish order and get the machinery of development into motion. The only central government that many of the new nations have known is that which was established by the colonial power, so that a period of transition is needed to enable the peoples of the new nation to work out their relationships.

Related to this problem of establishing a strong central government is the need for sufficient power to lead the nation in the very difficult and painful steps that are needed for economic development. The earnings of foreign trade and new industries have to be amassed into a capital fund to underwrite growth and cannot be spent immediately for consumer items. Government leaders do not feel that they can rely upon the seemingly slow and inefficient democratic process to make the crucial decisions that must be made.

But flexibility on matters such as politics, technology, education, and the mass media is an easy task in comparison with the difficulty of rethinking, altering, and in many ways relinquishing the Cold War mentality that has been so deeply instilled in Western people since World War II. Yet we must overcome this attitude if mankind's death struggle with global poverty is to be won.

Terms such as "Communist" and "anti-Communist" have often been used as smoke screens and thought-inhibitors by political spokesmen and those whom they represent. Not every revolutionary group is subservient to Moscow or Peking, and not every left-wing party or leader is revolutionary. Besides, some of the dictators billed as "noncommunist" have been proven such vicious oppressors that revolution against them is both justifiable and necessary. Robert Heilbroner claims that "the United States in recent years has thrown its support against *all* revolutions and provided its backing for *all* groups that have opposed revolutions, regardless of the merits of the one or the demerits of the other . . . ."[6] He calls for a more profound understanding of the dynamics of revolution:

> . . . when revolution comes, the leadership may spring from many sources other than Communist party membership. Angry and disillusioned army officers, idealistic middle-class intellectuals, even peasant guerrilla leaders, may provide the nuclei that seed the clouds of potential disaffection. . . . Thus revolution and communism are by no means synonymous, although it is undeniably true that Communists are working for and eager to lead a revolutionary thrust.
>
> Whatever the leadership, however, it is clear that some sort of authoritarian nationalist socialism will be the vehicle of change. Whether or not this socialism will become communist . . . depends on many [factors]. . . . The nationalism that

[6] *Ibid.,* p. 72.

is so powerful a motive force in revolutions tends to drive the leadership away
from communism because of its danger of vassalage to a great state; the need for
moral support and technical advice may drive it toward accepting or concocting
some version of the communist catechism.[7]

If a revolutionary nationalist socialism is necessary, as
Heilbroner claims, to achieve prompt economic
development, the benefit is most emphatically worth the
cost.

Even if we find it impossible to be in sympathy with
revolution or a one-party socialist state in an
underdeveloped nation, the immorality and the risks of
preventing the emergence of such governments by our own
military action or subversion are greater than the possible
evil of such governments. Vietnam should have made the
risks and costs of counter-revolutionary wars abundantly
evident to everybody. Nations cannot be forced prematurely
into a given form of government or the espousal of a given
political philosophy any more than an individual can or
should be coerced into a certain type of religious faith.

THE BIBLICAL WITNESS

All that has been said previously about the economic
immorality of individuals and the economic injustice
perpetrated by the ruling classes within one nation applies
with extra force to the international scene. The "widows and
orphans" whose mistreatment is particularly scandalous are
simply a larger percentage of the population in the Third
World, and the wrongs committed against them are merely
inflicted with even greater effectiveness on an even grander
scale.

The special theme of the biblical witness which must be
emphasized in this connection is the warning of national

[7] *Ibid.*, pp. 71-72.

punishment which is a part of the prophetic message concerning God's judgment. Not only individuals are to be held accountable and made to pay for their misdeeds; whole nations must from time to time be chastised by the rod of the Lord on account of their evil.

The famous prologue to the Book of Amos makes it absolutely clear that God's wrath will be discharged against *all* nations which are guilty of cruel violence, oppression, and exploitation of weaker nations:

> Thus says the Lord:
> "For three transgressions of Damascus,
>   and for four, I will not revoke the punishment;
> because they have threshed Gilead
>   with threshing sledges of iron. . . .
>
> ". . . of Gaza . . .
> because they carried into exile a whole people
>   to deliver them up to Edom. . . .
>
> ". . . of Tyre . . .
> because they delivered up a whole people to Edom,
>   and did not remember the covenant of brotherhood. . . .
>
> ". . . of Edom . . .
> because he pursued his brother with the sword,
>   and cast off all pity,
> and his anger tore perpetually,
>   and he kept his wrath for ever. . . .
>
> ". . . of the Ammonites . . .
> because they have ripped up women with child in Gilead,
>   that they might enlarge their border. . . .
>
> ". . . of Moab . . .
> because he burned to lime
>   the bones of the king of Edom. . . .
>
> ". . . of Judah . . .
> because they have rejected the law of the Lord,
>   and have not kept his statutes,
> but their lies have led them astray. . . .
>
> ". . . of Israel . . .
> because they sell the righteous for silver,

and the needy for a pair of shoes—
they that trample the head of the poor
into the dust of the earth,
and turn aside the way of the afflicted. . . ."
Amos 1 and 2

The catalog of iniquities would be somewhat different today, but we may be sure that a twentieth-century Amos would be every bit as specific about the nations and their atrocities:

Thus says the Lord:
"For three transgressions of Western Europe,
and for four, I will not revoke the punishment;
because they have colonialized whole continents,
forcing the people of Africa and Asia to bear the burden of the white man's
cruelty and greed under the pretext of 'taking up the white man's burden' . . .

". . . of the Soviet Union . . .
because they have slaughtered and deported and terrorized hundreds of thousands
in order to maintain their iron grip in Hungary and Czechoslovakia. . . .

". . .of the United States of America . . .
because they have used napalm in Vietnam and
'cast off all pity' at My Lai, and because they have made a whorehouse of
Havana and San Juan, and fattened their bellies in Brazil and Venezuela at the
expense of the people of those countries. . . ."

Moreover, the fury of the Lord's forthcoming punishment is described by the prophets in terms that are bloodcurdling even to readers of the century of Auschwitz and Hiroshima. The covenant people will not be utterly cast off ("How can I give you up, O Ephraim! How can I hand you over, O Israel! . . . My heart recoils within me, my compassion grows warm and tender." Hosea 11:8), but their sin is especially grievous. Their nation can no more escape the wages of sin than the surrounding nations can—and all of the groups of the offending power elites (including the churches!) will have to suffer retribution:

> ". . . on the day I punish Israel for his transgressions,
>> I will punish the altars of Bethel
>> and the horns of the altar shall be cut off
>> and fall to the ground
>> I will smite the winter house with the summer house;
>> and the houses of ivory shall perish.
>> and the great houses shall come to an end." says the Lord.
>
> (Amos 3:14-15; *cf.* Amos 1–3:2 and the whole array of parallel passages of doom in Isaiah, Jeremiah, Ezekiel, Joel, Zephaniah, Zechariah, Obadiah, and Malachi.)

Is there any reason to think that the "have" nations of the twentieth century can escape an equally devastating divine judgment on their wicked treatment of less powerful peoples? If and when the Third-World "man with the hoe" rises up in bloody revolution against his oppressors, what feeble words of self-justification will form on the mouths of rich Christians? Will we be able to stomach the unleashing of the full arsenal of biological, chemical, and nuclear weapons now standing ready in the fortresses of the technologically advanced countries, or must we not do all that we can to prohibit their use, even their preparation and stockpiling? If the relationship between the rich and poor nations cannot be reordered with justice for the poor and armed conflict does come, Christians must consider very thoughtfully what will be their stance. Will they join in the defense of their way of life as citizens of a rich nation, even though that way of life rests in part upon unjust and exploitative treatment of the poor nations? Does the cross place a different demand upon the followers of Jesus in such a situation? In the late sixties when some felt that armed rebellion by some black groups was a real threat, William Stringfellow defined the issue for Christians in terms which are relevant in this context of the struggle between the rich and poor nations. Stringfellow wrote:

Whenever it comes to pass that white men *who are Christians* [italics in original] are attacked by Negroes and endure ridicule or humiliation or interference or taunting torture; whenever it comes to pass that white Christians are exposed to the loss of their possessions, or status, or jobs, or property, or homes, or even families; if one's own life itself is at issue, let the witness of the white Christian—for himself, for all white men, and, in fact, for all men everywhere—be the witness of the Cross.

. . . there is *no other way* [italics in original] that this enormous, desperate, growing accumulation of guilt, shame, estrangement, and terror can be absolved. There never has been—for any man, anywhere, at any time—any other way. In the work of God in our midst, reconciling black men and white men, there is no escape from the Cross.[8]

There is no hope for economic justice in the world, no hope for prompt economic development in the "have not" nations, unless the people of the "have" countries are willing to live more sanely and share more generously than they ever have before. As the German theologian Helmut Gollwitzer has reminded us in his new book, *The Rich Christians and Poor Lazarus,* for the relatively affluent nations to insist on a continually escalating standard of living will doom both their souls and the very lives of the starving masses in the underdeveloped countries.[9] It might even cause the doom of the human race, for the resource depletion and pollution being caused by present production-consumption patterns and trends in the rich nations simply cannot continue without disastrous consequences for mankind's natural environment.

[8] William Stringfellow, *Dissenter in a Great Society* (Nashville: Abingdon Press by arrangement with Holt, Rinehart and Winston, 1966), p. 122.

[9] Helmut Gollwitzer, *The Rich Christians and Poor Lazarus,* trans. David Cairns (Edinburgh: St. Andrew Press, 1970), pp. 88-89.

7.
What
the
Individual
Can
Do

We now turn to a discussion of the kind of action which is needed to realize some of the ideals advanced in the first part of this book and to meet the problems which have been presented. This chapter will serve to help the individual face up to his own personal stewardship and witness.

How would you define personal stewardship? Each one of us has a little money to spend. Each one of us has some kind of work to do. Each one of us has been given a reasonable share of the rich resources in God's world. What are we going to do about all of these? Are we going to spend what we have responsibly? How are we going to perform our work whatever that may be? How are we going to care for what God has given? Do we really want to become involved in the efforts to reduce or even end injustice and poverty present in our own economic system? Do we really care about the plight of the millions of poor in the Third-World nations? It ought to be self-evident to Christians that discipleship is a full-time job that calls each follower of Jesus to exercise his best analytical and imaginative capacities in discovering *every possible means* of bearing effective witness in his personal life against the economic evils of our culture.

Perhaps the key text might be simply Jesus' words: "He who is not with me is against me" (Luke 11:23). Anyone who is not constantly examining his own life-style, his consumption patterns, his investments of money and energy, and, in short, all areas of his behavior to find new ways of fighting against injustice is not a wholehearted disciple. As certain leaders of the black poor have declared, "If you are not a part of the solution—really a *part* of it, *involved* with it, *committed* to it—you are a part of the problem."

We must discover how scriptural guidance about individual stewardship relates to corporate stewardship in the society at large. While there are few specific passages which deal with stewardship at this level, the overwhelming weight of the biblical witness proclaims the solidarity of the human community. We are created for steadfast covenant love of God and neighbor (Hosea 2:18-23; Matthew 22:36-40), and this central theme of biblical faith makes it impossible to use isolated proof texts to rationalize irresponsibility in social and corporate relationships.

Further, we cannot maintain that faith alone, in the sense of a set of intellectual affirmations or verbal formulae, is all there is to the Christian life:

> What does it profit, my brethren, if a man says he has faith but has not works? Can his faith save him? If a brother or sister is ill-clad and in lack of daily food, and one of you says to them, "Go in peace, be warmed and filled," without giving them the things needed for the body, what does it profit? So faith by itself, if it has no works, is dead (James 2:14-17).

Those who truly love the Lord and are deeply committed to his purpose in life will be constantly spending themselves unreservedly in the struggle to bring about reconciliation and justice in the human community. They may not necessarily be successful in this effort, for man's freedom also means the freedom to wreak havoc, even the total destruction of life on the planet. But Christian people will be unremittingly dedicated to the quest for more just social policies, and they will be using every ounce of energy and every grain of intelligence and imagination in their heads and hearts in the attempt to devise wise policies and get them implemented as rapidly and as effectively as possible.

There are at least five ways in which a responsible Christian can express his personal stewardship.

1. *Giving* money or other gifts through the church or trustworthy agencies, such as the Salvation Army, the United Fund, or Church World Service, is a good place to begin. Sharing in the form of gifts and love offerings is a *must*. Tithing in some form is an index of the sincerity of anyone who claims to be a fighter against economic injustice.

Tithing is a word that often brings a groan to the lips of many people. Nobody wants to be reminded that he is a sinner, but the minister who doesn't keep reminding his people of their responsibility is not executing his vocation faithfully. The generosity of the early Christians, who "sold their possessions and goods and distributed them to all" (see Acts 2:43-47), ought still to be a model for us. To be sure, if tithing is used in a legalistic way to avoid other demands, it is subject to the condemnation pronounced by Jesus upon the legalists of his own day:

> Woe to you, scribes and Pharisees, hypocrites! for you tithe mint and dill and cummin, and have neglected the weightier matters of the law, justice and mercy

and faith; these you ought to have done, without neglecting the others (Matthew 23:23).

At the same time, giving ought to be done intelligently. A church member has a right to object when the church budget is spent extravagantly. One must also devise ways of giving that do not impress upon the beneficiary his dependent status and his obligation to show proper deference and gratitude lest all generosity cease. The redistribution of wealth we call "charity" ought to be regarded as a matter of justice, not of generosity. The ultimate goal of the reforms involved in the quest for economic justice is not simply a redistribution of goods, but an equalization of power and status that abolishes the distinction between "generous giver" and "grateful beneficiary." The purposes served by a contribution and the agency to which it is given must be genuinely valid purposes. The quantity of money given to help a certain person or group must move toward dignified self-support as well as economic well-being. Gifts which help to promote a change in the institutionalized structures of society that make some people dependent on gifts by private individuals instead of entitled by law to an adequate level of welfare are even better than individual philanthropy of any kind. The efficient operation of the charitable institution is also a relevant criterion.

2. *Sharing* is a second type of personal stewardship that deserves far more use today. It was very common a hundred years ago and is coming back into widespread usage especially among the people of the counter culture.

Is it really necessary for a family to own everything it needs to use? Is it not sometimes an excessive demand for convenience or a desire for the power of individual autonomy that puts one or two cars in the garage of every family that can afford the purchase, a washing machine and a dryer in every laundry room, and so on? If more people could get over the ad-implanted notion that self-respect demands ownership and exclusive use whenever we want it and not a minute later, we might be able to free an enormous amount of money for better uses.

A side benefit certainly would be the increase in neighborliness that would normally follow from cooperative use of cars, appliances, machine tools, and sports equipment. But the people involved must have the kind of consciousness which does not make them feel that they are being imposed upon, but allows them to feel solid satisfaction in their thrift and intelligence. The great variety of communes springing up all over the country proves that people of all ages and outlooks can find a type of cooperative living arrangement which gives them the degree of privacy they want while enabling them to live more cheaply, elementally, and richly.[1] A return to sharing would represent a return to a pattern of generous co-humanity that was simply taken for granted in patriarchal times (Genesis 18:1-8) and the early Christian community (Acts 4:32-35).

3. *Investing* is another avenue of personal stewardship with endless possibilities for useful assistance to those who need it and can use it well. Responsible investing by Christians has two angles: the negative one of avoiding firms that engage in unethical practices or that produce a commodity or service one cannot conscientiously support; and the positive one of seeking worthy firms or individuals, especially those that might not be able to secure backing elsewhere.

The first aspect of responsible investment has little real

[1] Joseph Downing, "The Tribal Family and the Society of Awakening," in Herbert Otto, ed., *The Family in Search of a Future* (New York: Appleton-Century Crofts, 1970), pp. 119-135.

utility when practiced by an individual. That is to say, the sale or boycott of a given stock by an individual cannot have any significant impact on the corporation in question, and the value of the act has to be seen more in symbolic than strategic terms.

However, we should not despise symbolic actions. In the Bible such actions are described on many occasions as signs of the significance of encounters between God and man or between man and man. (See Genesis 28:18-22; Jeremiah 13:1-11; Mark 14:3-9). Even so, symbolic actions may sometimes be used to promote a sense of complacency or even self-righteousness. If this danger can be avoided, the symbolic act can have a double benefit—it helps to maintain the integrity of the individual who takes the action, and a wave of such actions may ignite a substantial movement that does bring about policy change. The lunch counter sit-ins of the early civil rights movement did not start out as carefully planned steps in a long-range strategy; they were merely symbolic expressions of the dignity of young men and women who were no longer willing to be humiliated by existing customs. Yet the movement mushroomed into a strategy that brought very significant results.

The other aspect of investment is the one which best lends itself to individual action. At the neighborhood or local level, there are thousands of worthwhile projects that need relatively small amounts of capital, the kind of money which could be put together by comparatively small groups of concerned people in a given locale. Consumer cooperatives enable low-income people to buy essential groceries and household supplies at prices often much lower than those in the supermarkets or the neighborhood stores. Small businessmen often need only a modest, short-term loan in order to make an improvement that will put them on a sound footing for years to come. Blacks and Puerto Ricans sometimes need only small additional funds to gain ownership of a ghetto store which would be far more acceptable to neighborhood folk, and far more serviceable to them, if owned by a resident. Integrated housing developments or apartments frequently need capital; indeed, there is a national organization whose purpose it is to secure a "tithing in investment" for nonrestricted housing in metropolitan areas where it is desperately needed. [2]

Why not explore opportunities for socially helpful investments in your own area, and then put together the amount needed by enlisting the participation of other church members or like-minded persons in the vicinity? This effort would have a double side benefit: it would put you in touch with poor people and/or blacks in your own locale and would thus open channels of communication across racial and class lines. It would also multiply your contacts with other churchgoers, thus helping to build some of the bridges of ecumenical understanding and cooperation that the church ought to have in our day and time.

4. *The stewardship of talents in work* is another important area for personal witness. Among the factors which deserve to be examined in this context are honesty, competence, alienation from one's job, humane working conditions, and the usefulness of the product or service. The responsibilities and opportunities of those who hold positions of policy-making authority or administrative power are also involved, but these aspects of stewardship will be discussed in the next two chapters on social change.

Honesty and competence are two economic virtues we ought to be able to take for granted, but unfortunately this is

---

[2] Information may be obtained by writing the National Committee Against Discrimination in Housing, 1865 Broadway, New York, NY 10023.

not the case. So many people have become accustomed to cheating in small ways or even big ones because "everybody else does it" that honesty is sometimes regarded as almost heroic. It certainly shouldn't be that way for the Christian. As for competence, it is the most underrated value in economic life. Competence is a form of honesty, for incompetence robs somebody of part of what he's paying for. Its costs in terms of money, frayed nerves, exasperation, and, finally, disgust and hatred, are incalculable.

Alienation and dehumanization in the work process are more difficult issues to analyze. The first may have to do simply with the "match" between a certain job and an individual's temperament or preferences. In cases of this kind, there is no serious moral principle involved. It is just a matter of switching to a job that has an atmosphere or a rhythm more in accord with one's likes and dislikes. But if alienation is the result of working conditions that are unsafe or unhealthy if engaged in for a long time, then grave moral questions are involved. The same is true of work which is so demanding that it turns the worker into a machinelike subhuman creature. In situations like this, merely quitting and finding another job for yourself is an ethical cop-out. The truly responsible thing for the Christian to do is to see dehumanized work as a public issue instead of just a personal woe and to organize others to bring about a change in the working conditions. While in some situations, an individual may see no other real alternative to withdrawing, he should be aware of the implications of his action. If another person is hired to take his place and accepts the unjust or inhumane working conditions, then what has been gained? The real challenge is to publicize the immoral aspects of the situation in order to bring about a change in it.

The most crucial questions of all, perhaps, are those

which arise in connection with the matter of putting out a genuinely useful product and selling it in an ethical manner. Honesty, competence, a pleasant work process, and delightful personnel relations cannot make up for an output which is destructive to those who consume it, or one which is relatively useless, inferior, or expensive in comparison with what could be produced and ought to be available for the satisfaction of real human need. Many persons of conscience find it impossible to work on certain kinds of research, or to help make a product they think people shouldn't buy anyhow, or to keep on overlooking skewed priorities and shoddy product features, such as planned obsolescence.

And of course the same considerations apply to selling. Isn't it unethical to try to get a man to buy something he really doesn't need at a price you know he can't afford to pay? While the buyer has to be the final judge of what he wants and can afford, the salesman has an obligation to insure that the buyer is aware of all the appropriate factors that need to be considered (including the availability of alternative models with other features at another price, and the performance and durability of the commodity being considered). Brotherly concern about the customer or the client is the "second mile" we are called upon to go in addition to the first mile of honesty and competency (see Matthew 5:38-42).

5. *Consumer behavior* is the area of personal stewardship that will probably be most interesting to the average person. The most basic general principle that is capable of being advanced here is a reiteration of all that has been said so far in this chapter: try to support those products, firms, and specific economic policies which meet genuine human needs effectively through humane working conditions at the lowest reasonable price. If one fully understands and acts

upon this principle, his actions as a consumer will follow ethical lines.

A product is morally suspect if it possesses any of the following characteristics:

• The consequences of its use are demonstrably destructive to individuals, to community life, or to the environment. This would include any excessive use of drugs, alcohol, and tobacco. DDT and non-biodegradable containers should also be avoided. Automobiles would not be condemned *per se,* but surely one ought to withhold support from ridiculously high-powered chrome-bedecked monsters and support sanity in design and cost by buying smaller or less ecologically damaging cars.

• Its advertising appeals to unworthy motives, such as the pride of conspicuous consumption, lasciviousness, and mindless superficiality in leisure pursuits (see Matthew 6:25-33). Objectionable ads ought to elicit complaints, so that they will be withdrawn and their damaging effects can be ended as soon as possible.

One way of registering objections is to send protests in the postage-paid envelopes often provided with direct-mail advertising. If enough people make the advertiser pay return postage, he will begin to notice the complaints! Letters of explanation should be sent to firms whose products or advertising are being resisted so that the management officials will know how to interpret sales resistance. These letters do not have to be unpleasant, either. One can write quite matter-of-factly, "I won't buy this product because... , but I would be interested in a product like . . ." or "Your product is good enough to sell on its own merits. Why not advertise it directly instead of appealing to the less-worthy instincts aimed at in such a disgusting ad?"

• The manufacturer is known to be guilty of

paying unfair wages, having plants with dehumanizing working conditions, pressuring sales personnel so intensely that they are driven to pressure prospective customers, and the like.

The Bible says that one should be a good steward. Stewardship is the way of life for the sincere and committed Christian. Each and every one of us has a responsibility not only to give as we are able, but also to do responsible work, to handle the earth's resources responsibly, to take care of our own property and neighborhood in a responsible manner, and to spend money intelligently and wisely for those things which will bring us the most fulfillment and at the same time meet the standards of economic justice for everyone.

8.
Strategies for Changing Institutions

We can understand better the need for institutional change if we look at another part of our life. During the decades of the 1950's and 1960's, many persons of goodwill went through changes in their attitudes and actions regarding race relations. They were never really bigoted persons. They always tried to treat others equally, and they always deplored the derogatory remarks and the unfair treatment given to many blacks in our society. But before the passage of civil rights laws and the efforts, both official and unofficial, of public and private institutions to eliminate discrimination, the goodwill of individuals was probably rather impotent. They were never sure what to say, when they could say it, or to whom, and so they found themselves silent and paralyzed when they saw a black being turned away from a restaurant, a hotel, a school, or a job.

With the changed climate of opinion and the changed laws of recent years, individuals of goodwill have a much better opportunity to be effective. Now, when they see a black being given the runaround or passed over for some opportunity for which he is entitled to be considered, they can speak up with confidence to support his claim to equal treatment. *It's against the law* now to refuse equal access to public accommodations. *It's against company policy* to hire and promote only whites. *It's even considered bad citizenship and bad manners* not to be as polite and friendly to blacks as one would be to anyone else in similar circumstances.

The moral is clear: personal kindness and goodwill need the support of a legal and institutional framework if they are to be operative for the benefit of the disadvantaged.

What is true in the fight for racial justice is equally true in the quest for economic justice—maybe more so, in view of the fact that economic injustice is often more hidden and more pervasive than racism. Individual philanthropy and honesty can never do more than scratch the surface. The numbers and the misery of the poor will continue to increase if individual stewardship is all that is practiced. Until and unless concerned individuals join together for effective action in the governmental jurisdictions, the offices and factories where they are employed, and the network of neighborhood associations to which they belong, economic injustice will continue to reign. Christians simply *must* learn to think in terms of institutional and societal policy goals, and to act collectively on carefully planned social change strategies.

To many people this assertion about the need for strategic sophistication and organized, collective political activity in one's union, corporation, or civic club, as well as in local, state, and federal governments, is a counsel of despair. Some have never considered the proposition that Christian discipleship in our day demands such efforts. Those who have recognized the need for such action may never have been able to "find a handle" and do anything of this kind.

Some church people have tried and been roundly discouraged by their almost total failure to achieve any success. But fortunately the burden does not fall entirely on the shoulders of politically inexperienced church members. There are many persons of wisdom and conscience in positions of leadership in political and economic organizations at every level. Part of our responsibility as ordinary citizens is simply to be able to discern the probable consequences of various proposals set before the public or other bodies where we have some kind of vote or influence, so that we shall know what to support and what to oppose. This chapter will suggest some of the most promising policies which will help to overcome the principal causes of economic injustice.

A STRATEGY PLANNING CHART

Look at the chart on pages 94 and 95. In the first column headed "Problem Diagnosis" there is a comparison between the factors of economic injustice attributed to the culture of poverty and those caused by the economic power groups. This listing pinpoints the dimensions of the evil that can be readily identified and attacked.

In the second column "Policy Goals"—what needs to be done to remedy the evil—are suggested as solutions for specific aspects of the problem.

In the next column on the right under "Church Objectives" are illustrations of specific tasks for church members. Here you will find illustrations of the kind of

A STRATEGY
PLANNING
CHART
AGAINST
ECONOMIC
INJUSTICE:

Problem Diagnosis	Policy Goals

The culture of poverty:
 	
Educational handicaps
Deficient skills
 	
Health care
 	
Attitudes
	Improved general
	   education
	Improved vocational
	   education
	Urban orientation centers
	
	Free basic health care for all
	   citizens
	
	Increased cross-cultural contact

**Concentration of
economic power:**
 	
1. **Maldistribution of
   economic resources**
   Money
   Jobs
	Job creation
	Minimum wage extension
	Unionization
	Guaranteed annual income

2. **Poor housing and
neighborhoods:**
 	
   Housing
   Neighborhood life
	Public housing
	Rent supplements
	Loans for home
	   ownership by the poor
	Improved public services
	   (garbage, streets, police,
	   transportation)

3. **Misplaced priorities:** Hidden subsidies for the "haves" Present tax laws Pricing Marketing	Elimination of subsidies for rich Tax reform legislation Ombudsmen to protect consumers and borrowers Wage and price controls Restrictions on advertising Fair trade laws and aid policies Technology assessment

Church Objectives	Targets	Tactics
Tutorial programs for dropouts and slow learners Pressure exerted on school boards and systems A community-focused adult education program Free clinic at the church, using time donated by physicians, dentists, and nurses Study groups, action projects, and worship activities that cross racial and class lines	Textbook publishers School system administrators Teachers, professional associations Parents Pupils Hospital boards and administrators Doctors' and nurses' professional associations	Boycotts Demonstrations Dialogue Gathering relevant information Community organization Personal example and conversation
Opening up jobs in church establishments and agencies Mobilizing church constituencies for lobbying Study groups and intensive dialogue with key individuals	Policy makers in religious institutions Legislators and anyone who has influence with them Churchgoers, opinion makers, employers, and the like	Dialogue Visits, letters, pressure of various kinds Informational and educational program, personal visits
Sponsor nonprofit housing construction Organize churchgoing bankers, builders, and landlords to set up loan funds to provide more housing for poor	Department of Housing and Urban Development Landlords and bankers who are Christians	Secondary strategy Dialogue
Participate in lobbying campaigns Mobilize church people to protest bad advertising and abuses in government policies and program administration Organize unofficial ombudsmen from church talent Stockholder lawsuits	Voters and their elected officials Consumers and retail store managers Lawyers, experienced government employees, and the like Corporation policy makers	Mass media appeals Speakers Door-to-door canvassing Study groups Dialogue Pressure

action that church people—a social concerns committee, a congregation, an ecumenical body, or simply a group of Christians acting on their own without official ecclesiastical sponsorship—may execute especially well to help achieve or consolidate some of the policy goals.

The last two columns are labeled "Targets" and "Tactics." The first refers to the persons and/or institutions which must be persuaded or pressured to do certain things if the goals are to be achieved. The second suggests some means that may be used to get these "targets" to act.

BREAKING THE "CULTURE OF POVERTY" CYCLE

Policies designed to remedy personal and subcultural traits which are, from the standpoint of the dominant society, "deficiencies" are fraught with ambiguities. On the one hand, society certainly has a right and a responsibility to see to it that every citizen has a chance to learn certain skills and values considered necessary for membership in it. Thus, the public school system is expected to teach all children the rudimentary knowledge of "readin', writin', and arithmetic" and the habits of punctuality, honesty, sobriety, and diligence that they will need to get jobs and be good employees in urban society. Employers have a right to expect these skills and habits in job applicants, and applicants who do not have them have no reasonable right to complain if they have difficulty in obtaining or holding jobs.

But there is another side to the matter. Perhaps society has demanded more conformity than it needed or had a right to demand, thus threatening the sense of ethnic identity and the retention of certain highly valued subcultural behavior patterns that are very precious to many persons. Black parents may have reason to be worried about the "brainwashing" being given to their children in white-oriented and white-dominated schools.

Rebellious actions are symptoms of a deep cultural and political crisis in the United States. The rebels seem to be saying, "We want our fair share in return for our labor in this industrial society, but we don't want to be a part of it, and we absolutely refuse to be like you." Understandably enough, the reaction of mainstream Americans is often to say, "Well, all right then, if you won't meet our requirements, you're certainly not going to enjoy the benefits of our system!" But these two positions, maintained in an unqualified way, would lead to a truly disastrous polarization of the populace and periodic outbreaks of conflict so savage as to endanger civilized existence. Must not both sides make some concessions? Do not both sides need to appreciate realistically the contribution that people with somewhat different values and personal styles can make to them?

Insofar as the culture of poverty is a crippling vise which limits the aspirations and even the imaginations of the poor to such an extent that they actually have no free choice in determining their own identity, it ought to be called into question and changed. If job opportunities are truly opened up, if demeaning social barriers are torn down, and if health and education facilities are bettered to the point that poor people *can* develop the skills in demand and go through the newly opened doors, most of them *will* do so. But so long as what Harrington calls "the vicious circle of poverty" remains unbroken, so long as lack of opportunity and discrimination cause low income, in turn

which causes bad housing and bad health, in turn

which cause low energy levels, mental illness, family conflict and instability, delinquency and crime, in turn which cause a poor response to (usually inadequate or inappropriate) educational opportunities, in turn

which causes low job qualifications, in turn

which cause low income—

then the culture of poverty will be reinforced as a defense mechanism which offers some kind of desperate protection against the psychological, social, and economic ravages of the "System."[1]

The government and other powerful institutions of our society do not have a right to use the public education system to brainwash minority group children, or the public health and welfare agencies to whip the poor into line. But they do have an obligation to equalize the opportunity structures which are at present so unequal and are therefore responsible in such large measure for perpetuating poverty.

If the poor at least have a genuine choice, most of them will probably opt for meaningful membership in the society. There will of course be many different styles and degrees of substantial membership, many different combinations of straight job performance mixed with Afro-American or Spanish-American or Appalachian leisure-time pursuits and personal styles of appearance. But there will be enough conformity on essential values, and enough freedom on nonessentials, to make our society healthily pluralistic instead of dangerously fragmented and polarized.

Some of the following policy goals are of decisive importance:

[1] Michael Harrington, *The Other America* (New York: The Macmillan Company, 1962), pp. 15-17.

• *Improved general education.* Increasingly rapid technological change will probably make job obsolescence more common than in the past. Many analysts favor education in "how to keep on educating yourself the rest of your life" over specific training of any kind. This kind of education is far more difficult to carry out, but its helpfulness would obviously be unsurpassed if it can be successfully designed and implemented. Both general and vocational education must be available to adults as well as to children and youth.

• *Improved vocational education.* Some circles tend to scorn the value of vocational education. But as long as the training is not for obsolete jobs or jobs that do not pay a living wage, and as long as the jobs for which training is given offer dignity and reasonable security, this will furnish just the kind of opportunity desired by many members of the labor force.

• *Urban orientation centers.* Many of the needs of poor people, especially those in the cities, are emotional rather than intellectual. These needs may range from the mild and temporary confusion or discouragement of the newcomer to the severe cultural shock of someone who has become totally disoriented, or even psychologically disturbed, by his experiences in the city. Meeting these needs effectively is a very difficult task. Many of those who could benefit most from the help of a social worker or a poverty lawyer will not go near a settlement house or a legal-aid clinic. It is not enough to make the needed services available in a formal sense. They must be made practically available through personnel who know a certain neighborhood well and are capable of establishing enough rapport to know where to look and how to reach or open themselves for contact with the persons whom they can serve.

• *Improved health services.* One of the great scandals of our scientifically advanced civilization is the exclusion of the poor from its medical care. Even free medical clinics sometimes go unused in poor neighborhoods because of mistrust or sheer lack of information. Two specific kinds of health care for the poor are of crucial importance: therapy for drug users and birth-control clinics for those who want such help.

HUMANIZING THE ECONOMIC POWER COMPLEX

If the most important cause of poverty is the concentration of economic power, the most important policy goals for its alleviation are those leading to reform of the abuses of "business as usual" in the major political and economic institutions of the society. Since the maldistribution of economic goods is at the heart of the problem, that's a good place to begin our catalog of top priority goals.

1. **Measures intended to increase the earning and/or buying power of the poor:**

• *Job creation.* One of the revolutionary economic theories being more generally accepted is the idea that no government ever needs to allow another great depression. It can always pump money into the economy and create the demand which would create jobs in the private sector of the economy by creating jobs and paying for them with deficit spending in the public sector. From this realization grows the notion that government policy should be to keep unemployment quite low at all times, even if government becomes "the employer of last resort."

The apparent folly of WPA-type jobs has been the butt of many jokes. But if it can be shown that the society stands in urgent need of services that could be rendered by public sector jobs *which could furnish employment for two or three million of the citizens who most need it,* then the idea of government job creation has overwhelming merit.[2]

That is exactly the situation in the United States at the present time. Many of the most grievous lacks in public service characteristic of our depleted society exist in geographical and occupational areas where poor people are best qualified to operate effectively. This match between the demand for services and the supply of persons best equipped to render them has created a proposal for "new careers for the poor" in para-professional roles in fields such as teaching, medical care, tending children, rehabilitating inmates of penal institutions and the like. These occupational openings would be *careers* instead of merely *jobs,* because they would offer a chance for continuing growth in competence and promotion, say from "nurse's aid" to "medical assistant" to "doctor's associate," for example. They would offer growing dignity and status as well as income to people whose skills are very much needed as a complement to the highly specialized and limited skills of middle-class professional people who have little experience in dealing with the clients whom they are supposed to help.

 • *Extension of minimum wage coverage.* Millions of low-skill workers, who really need protection most, are not covered by the minimum wage legislation that builds an income floor under many relatively unskilled workers. This inequity is largely the result of abuses of power in the form of racial discrimination and lobbying. Extending the income floor under the feet of *all* members of the labor force would go a long way toward overcoming some of the economic

---

[2] See Arthur Pearl and Frank Riessman, *New Careers for the Poor* (New York: The Free Press, 1965).

injustice that afflicts several million such workers today.

• *Unionization.* Many Christians have supported organized labor's drive for recognition. They have seen it as a countervailing force which could bring fairer wages and better working conditions to laborers who otherwise would be taken advantage of by their employers.

Labor unions have been successful in some trades and industries, but millions of blue-collar workers are still not unionized and they are frequently exploited unjustly. They need the powers and benefits of collective bargaining just as badly as the steelworkers and automobile workers did fifty years ago.

• *Guaranteed annual income.* Spokesmen of many different positions on the political spectrum now seem agreed on the desirability of some simplified, nationally standardized guaranteed income to replace the crazy quilt of state laws on public welfare now in operation. A five-year experiment in New Jersey shows that many of the fears about the unwholesome consequences do not materialize. Recipients are not demoralized. People with decent, and decently remunerative, jobs do not quit work in order to pick up the dole. Considering the benefits of the program, its costs are less than those of comparable welfare programs.[3]

2. **Measures designed to improve the housing situation and neighborhood life of the poor:**

• *Public housing.* One of the most direct ways of insuring that the poor have a decent place to live is to provide public housing. The plan has often been badly designed and badly administered, even in those cases where adequate

---

[3] Information may be obtained by writing to Dr. Harold Watts, Irving Fisher Research Professor of Economics, The Cowles Foundation for Research in Economics, Yale University, New Haven, Connecticut 06520.

funds have been appropriated and the housing actually has been constructed without miles of red tape and years of delay. But flaws in previous public housing developments should not be used as an argument against the very idea. The way to remedy the existing faults is to have better design, better administration, and better human relations management in the public housing built. Much more housing could and should be built promptly.

• *Rent supplements.* Such supplements would make it possible to put poor people into available housing immediately. They make up the difference between a family's ability to pay and the market price of a home or an apartment. Rent supplements yield a side benefit, too. They often introduce a minority group family into a previously all-white neighborhood under circumstances that maximize their chances for friendly acceptance.

• *Legislation promoting home ownership for the poor.* This is another device for enabling some families who couldn't otherwise afford it to have good housing. In cases where loans and/or insurance would be beyond the financial reach of a family with a steady but limited income, the low-interest loans and guaranteed insurance provisions of this type of legislation are decisively helpful.

• *Improved public services.* We recognize that certain public services are essential as stimuli to and reinforcements for motivation to proper maintenance of a dwelling. No one wants to take the trouble to fix up his dwelling if he knows that the surrounding environment will remain smelly and ugly or unsafe. Adequate garbage service, streets that are well cared for, trustworthy police protection, sufficient transportation facilities, and attractive recreational areas are necessary to support investment of money and energy in good housing.

3. Measures intended to shift the priorities in the spending of public funds:

• *Termination of hidden subsidies to the rich.* Some examples of this were mentioned in Chapter 5. The best way to put an end to these subsidies is to limit the power of the corporations who are able to influence government policies in their favor. This method would be much more effective than a piecemeal approach involving lawsuits and exposés concerning specific outrages.

• *Plugging of tax loopholes.* Everyone knows that present tax laws favor the wealthy person and discriminate against the poor. More emphasis should be placed on progressive taxes like steep inheritance taxes and the graduated income tax rather than on regressive measures such as the sales tax. Once again, reform on the specific tax laws will require revision of the laws and customs governing the operation of most legislative bodies, state and national. At present many powerful legislators have a vested interest in the laws they have enacted and will not allow reforms to pass.

• *Ombudsmen.* Several other countries have had remarkable success with the appointment of watchdog personnel called "ombudsmen," the Swedish title of this post. An ombudsman's task is to receive and review complaints from individual citizens about the treatment they receive under government programs of aid or assistance. If the complainant has been unfairly denied the full amount of his pension, a chance to secure public housing, or something of the kind, corrective action will be taken immediately under the order of the ombudsman.

• *Consumer protection laws.* The first kind of law that comes to mind in this connection is legal sanction against loan frauds, high-pressure sales techniques involving deception, invasion of privacy, and the like. A more realistic approach to the magnitude of the problem will lead sooner or later to curbs on trickery in packaging and advertising.[4]

• *Technology assessment.* If we are to move from mere prevention of irrational waste or pollution and deception and cheating to more positive mechanisms for planning the wisest priorities, schedules, and methods for meeting the real human needs of all members of the commonwealth, some type of technology assessment process must be found. Many people do not want to see another federal agency set up for this purpose. Some observers favor what lawyers call "the adversary process," which would call for a semi-legal hearing on every major technological innovation envisaged. Proponents would be able to point out all foreseeable advantages, and opponents would alert the public to all conceivable risks. The resulting decision would result from a weighing of the contribution to society and optimal control of the dangerous side effects of the new technology.

Obviously the strategy sketched in this chapter is merely illustrative. Each group of concerned Christians will have to analyze the problem as it exists in their setting to figure out exactly which dimensions of it need to be attacked, what things need to happen, and how to make these things happen with the resources they can command. The important thing is to find a place to attack and to get started!

[4] Ralph Nader's Center for the Study of Responsive Law has done an excellent job of muckraking in this area. See, e.g., James S. Turner, *The Chemical Feast* (New York: Grossman Publishers, 1970).

9.
Tactics
for
Changing
Institutions

Several years ago, a group of church members in Southern California attempted to carry out an exceedingly ambitious lobbying program intended to get the congressmen of the area to vote against further atmospheric testing of nuclear weapons. The announcement of the campaign elicited an unusually gratifying response. Hundreds of church people in more than sixty communities agreed to participate in the six weeks of study that were to precede action. The quality of participation revealed a seriousness of commitment that was nothing less than thrilling. Participants did their homework faithfully. By the end of the study period they could quote radiation statistics and explain the precedents in legislative and diplomatic history which made congressional action on the issue proper as well as urgent.

But something happened on the way to Congress: Half of

those who had studied so faithfully within the walls of the church educational buildings suddenly found that they had no more time to give to the project. Most of those who remained found that they were strangely tongue-tied when it came to persuading the legislators. They were especially inept when it came to answering the congressmen's practical objections about the riskiness of the vote they were being asked to make. The church people had so little experience in talking with politicians that they felt hopelessly insecure and inadequate to the task of influencing them realistically on a concrete issue. They were so frightened by the prospect of making fools of themselves that they either dropped out or did a poor job of stating their case. The point is that *the best of intentions and the most serious preliminary study of complex issues leading to the finest of policy goals are wasted unless strategic "know how" and tactical follow-through can be practiced effectively.* To formulate wise goals without cultivating strategic cunning and tactical skill is the modern social action equivalent of "putting one's hand to the plow and looking back" (see Luke 9:62).

In this chapter we shall be talking about identifying targets and selecting appropriate tactics to use in helping to overcome economic injustice in our national life. (See the Strategy Planning Chart in the previous chapter.)

IDENTIFYING TARGETS

Target identification is essential. Unless one knows where the power lies and how it operates, one will not know where or how to apply pressure for change. He will therefore risk frittering away his limited energies in useless ways. Community power structure studies have revealed that elected officials, chairmen of the board of directors of a corporation, or other occupants of official positions of authority are often only "front men" for real wielders of power who like to stay behind the scenes.[1] In situations of this kind, the interests and vulnerabilities of the real power holders need to be discovered and appealed to or attacked.

Pinpointing targets realistically is particularly important for church agencies or social action groups, for their power base is apt to be very limited and thus their ability to exert pressure on high-ranking targets may be almost totally absent. Yet the potential power of the church's witness is great with certain persons and groups, especially in certain parts of the country. "Church power" was probably decisive in bringing about the passage of the Civil Rights Bill of 1964.[2] Thus, white middle-class church members should probably spend less time in the ghetto organizing a black neighborhood than they should in dialogue with other white middle-class people who make policy in the white institutions where they themselves live and work. Church social change agents should be particularly effective with targets who find it difficult to be indifferent to the moral arguments of Christians and the body of public opinion they represent.

In the struggle for economic justice, the most significant targets are the poor themselves, policy-makers in industry and government, labor leaders, and the leadership of other institutions which supply something vital to the economic processes. Some examples of such support groups are universities, research laboratories, and the professional associations that set standards for scientists and engineers. The leaders and constituencies of all voluntary associations

[1] See especially Floyd Hunter, *Community Power Structure* (Chapel Hill: The University of North Carolina Press, 1953) and Nelson W. Polsby, *Community Power and Political Theory* (New Haven: Yale University Press, 1963).

[2] Henry Clark, *The Irony of American Morality* (New Haven, Conn.: College and University Press, 1971), pp. 85-95.

which sometimes take an interest in wages, prices, the quality of goods and services available, and related matters may also be important. The likely places to look for the real exercise of power include any part of a process where information is obtained or exchanged, where money is appropriated or distributed, and where policies and schedules are set.

TACTICS

Any type of speech or action designed to influence what a target does may be considered a tactic. So literally any conversation, or even the symbolic "statements" made by modes of personal appearance and overall style of life, can be part of a social change strategy. Indeed, the social change agents who are most effective are often those who seem to be "on duty" every waking hour of every day, persons whose very presence is a reminder to the conscience that one is not doing all he might do as a disciple of Jesus Christ. In a sense, then, *personal example and personal conversation* are the most important tactics, the always available and always potentially useful tactics of the dedicated change agent. One does not have to be self-righteous or self-defeatingly "high-pressure" in carrying out personal witness. If one is truly filled with grace, he will be gracious in his dealings with others, and even unpleasant truths can be spoken in a quality of love that does not block communication.

But the very term "tactics" implies planned collective action. This can range from face-to-face *dialogue* in many forms (study groups, task forces, bargaining teams) and in many different moods (from stimulation to confrontation to pressure), to *educational campaigns* aimed at a fairly broad segment of public opinion, to *lobbying* directly with people who have both formal authority and real decision-making power, to *nonviolent direct action* of the kind made familiar during the civil rights movement of the early sixties. The best way to explain these is to show how they might be used with particular targets in social action strategies for the attainment of certain goals that are crucial in securing economic justice.[3]

CHANGING AN EDUCATIONAL SYSTEM

If one dimension of the problem of poverty is the culture of poverty, and if one crucial policy goal in overcoming this is an improved educational system, then a strategy for change in public schools is of the utmost importance. The strategic analysis that follows can be applied to any similar institution, for the key targets in a public education system have their obvious counterparts in many other institutions.

A long-range attack upon the inadequacies of the public school system would call for a drive on targets like the manufacturers of textbooks, who exert an enormous amount of influence on what is actually communicated to children, the professional associations whose standards and philosophical assumptions are reflected in textbooks, the teachers' colleges and graduate schools where classroom and administrative personnel receive their intellectual and psychological formation, the architects who design school buildings, the politicians who appropriate funds, the party leaders and lobbyists who influence them, and a host of others who have some input into the educational "product" that is offered to the pupils and parents who are consumers. But a short-range strategy can focus on just four groups: teachers, administrators, students, and parents.

[3] For a more complete explanation of the conceptual approach to strategy planning see Henry Clark, *Ministries of Dialogue* (New York: Association Press, 1971).

• Dialogue ought to work with *teachers* if it will work with anybody. Their training and their convictions are supposed to make them more responsive to facts and rational arguments. If they are not too exhausted from their classroom ordeals or too overworked and harried as a result of a moonlighting job they have taken to supplement their often skimpy paychecks, many teachers may be willing to participate in a carefully structured study of issues in public education, and responsive to the ideas and/or action implications that emerge. Lobbying in the form of an exchange of support may be possible if the group urging teachers to welcome subprofessional aides from the low-income community is large enough to offer substantial backing for the pay-raise campaign of teachers.

• *Students* also should respond to dialogue if teachers have been successful in transmitting rational values to them. Students are important as a target group to be mobilized in favor of desired goals, for their wishes are very important to many teachers, and their acceptance is essential to the optimal success of any changes instituted.

• Many *parents* will be open to influence through dialogue, and those who fit this description will be among the most valuable allies a proposed innovation can have. Others may be reached through some of the community-organizing techniques sketched below.

• *Administrators* may be the toughest targets to reach. They are probably more sensitive to the pressures emanating from the budgetary office of the state government than they are to any other considerations. They have to be sensitive to political and monetary factors, because if they are not, educational services will be cut back and children may be hurt by their loss. If good communications and trust can be established, an administrator often can be pressured by secondary strategy involving political figures or by direct action involving students and parents without alienating or damaging him. The administrator who sees the desirability of a certain change but feels his hands are tied may welcome pressure. He may try to convey his desire for it "between the lines" of his official statements.

NEIGHBORHOOD COMMUNITY ORGANIZATION

There are those who doubt that social change on behalf of the poor can take place or be effective from "the top down." They don't believe the poor can benefit from change unless they win it through the development and exercise of their own power. Such theorists believe that neighborhood community organization is the top priority tactical approach.

The prime goal of community organization is the attainment of power and self-consciousness on the part of the dispossessed. Specific goals cannot always be stated in advance. The people themselves will decide what they want as they grow in self-consciousness, and whatever they decide they want is worth pursuing. The initial targets are the indigenous leaders to whom these people look for guidance in their neighborhood—a barber, a minister, a pool shark, a candy-store operator, the top man in a youth gang, for example. The key points of the tactical path could best be described as follows:

- Organizers . . . filter through the neighborhood, asking questions and, more important, listening . . . wherever people are talking—to discover the residents' specific grievances:
- At the same time, the organizers try to spot the individuals and the groups on which people seem to lean for advice or to which they go for help: a barber, a minister, a mailman, a restaurant owner, etc., the "indigenous" leaders;
- The organizers get these leaders together, discuss the irritations, frustrations, and problems animating the neighborhood, and suggest the ways in which power might be used to ameliorate or solve them;

• A demonstration or series of demonstrations are put on to show how power can be used. These may take a variety of forms: a rent strike against slum landlords, a cleanup campaign against a notorious trouble spot, etc. What is crucial is that meetings and talk, the bedrock on which middle-class organizations founder, are avoided; the emphasis is on action, and on action that can lead to visible results. [4]

LOBBYING FOR A NEW LAW OR NEW ORGANIZATIONAL POLICIES

One of the main criticisms leveled against neighborhood organization is that it is too localistic. It deals with the immediate surface grievances of a particular local group, to the neglect of larger issues and basic causes of the symptoms attacked. Those who launch this criticism are usually in favor of seeking a permanent, overarching remedy to all present and future symptoms of the same kind by getting a law passed against them. The details of lobbying for a new law vary from legislature to legislature, but the main elements of this strategy are explained in any standard textbook on American politics. [5]

Similar techniques are used in seeking policy changes in any large organization. The man or woman who occupies a position of influence or policy-making authority in his job can sometimes strike a significant blow for justice simply by using his power in any one of the following ways:

_____ lower a price

_____ do away with an objectionable ad or sales practice

_____ improve the quality of a certain product or service

_____ eliminate something useless or shoddy

_____ raise wages

_____ make a more honest tax return

[4] Charles E. Silberman, *Crisis in Black and White* (New York: Random House, Inc., 1964), p. 327.

[5] See, for example, V. O. Key, *Politics, Parties and Pressure Groups*, 5th ed. (New York: Thomas Y. Crowell Co., 1964), pp. 128-161.

_____ stop discriminating against blacks in hiring, firing, and promoting or in union membership and opportunity structures.

At the very least, we can all protest or even refuse to carry out unjust policies at the level where we work.

Changing the system will get done only if those in authority are persuaded to make the changes in question. Sometimes information is all they need; if so, supply it. Usually something more needs to be done than dropping the needed information into a suggestion box or filing a routine memo. Effective communication may require getting a highly respected individual or committee to report on the issue in a challenging way. Sometimes an informal task force of people with similar values will have to work behind the scenes for some time to gather all the facts needed to make the case for change persuasively to a policy-setting person or group. Sometimes reform from within is so unlikely that embarrassing information may have to be leaked out to outsiders, who will then force the organization to change a bad practice.

INDIVIDUAL AND LOCAL INITIATIVE

In the final analysis, the details of strategy planning and execution are the responsibility of committed individuals working together at the local level. Each Christian must decide, thoughtfully and prayerfully, exactly what God calls him to do at a given moment in a given situation. Not every church member can take a vigorous role in social action designed to overcome the political and institutional causes of economic injustice. Not everyone is equipped with the skills, the temperament, or the fortitude to be effective in carrying out the tactics of social change strategy. But probably many more of us need to beware of deciding too quickly that this type of Christian discipleship is not a part of our calling.

Perhaps the situation is analogous to that described in the parable of the widow's mite (Mark 12:42-44).

   • No one would think of scoffing at the widow's mite. To give all you have is a noble and beautiful act, and the size of the gift doesn't matter in appreciating the spirit which prompted it.

   • On the other hand, it doesn't make sense to praise the wealthy man for giving a mite. To give practically nothing, when you could share generously, is an irresponsible act. The gift may be only a tiny fraction of what could and ought to be given.

There may be some who for various reasons cannot move beyond personal stewardship. If the often heavy demands of social change strategy exceed their abilities, they should not be blamed for holding back. But if a person has a great deal to give in political and institutional reform—years of experience in dealing with people, unbounded vigor, hours of relatively unscheduled time, a variety of talents, and intelligence—such a person cannot be satisfied with personal stewardship alone.

All of us can surely find some new ways of personal witness and stewardship in the Christian war against economic injustice. And isn't it also likely that most of us, even if we shy away from involvement in corporation, union, government, or neighborhood struggles, can find some task to perform in a church group's effort to attain some important objective? We all feel powerless at times. Economic justice will not come all at once, but we should at least try to do all we can in the struggle.

In our day and time, two of the most critically needed

virtues are the complementary traits of imagination and determination. We often think of these traits as polar opposites, but maybe this assumption bears reexamination. It is interesting, at any rate, that certain memorable passages of Scripture used to show the importance of one can also be interpreted as a recommendation of the other.

When the Sermon on the Mount enjoins us, for example, to go the second mile and be willing to give our cloak as well as our coat to one who asks for it (see Matthew 5:38-42), we usually think of perseverance as the virtue being commended. So it is—but is it not also possible to see in such passages an appeal to sensitivity and imagination, the kind of sensitivity and imagination present-day Christians must exercise if they are going to be able to formulate policies and devise tactics adequate to the staggering difficulties presented by the fight against economic injustice? We have to think of solutions never dreamed of before, and then we have to pursue them with a degree of ingenuity and determination seldom exhibited in the past.

We will be sure to encounter many latter-day Pharisees who will try to tell us that the policies suggested and the tactics employed are "unreasonable," "unprecedented," "improper," "not feasible" or even "outrageous." We must never be blind to well-founded criticism. But sometimes we will have to be imaginative and tough-minded enough to give the same kind of answer Jesus gave when he said, "The sabbath was made for man, not man for the sabbath" (Mark 2:27). The legal precedents, the customary procedures, and the "rules of the game" in organizational and political life are supposed to serve human beings. If they do not serve *all* of the people, *new* laws and practices must be elaborated, and vigorous means within moral limits are necessary and justifiable in pursuit of them.

10.
A New Perspective for the Good Life— and a Time for Decision

We have been considering some of the problems that face us as Christians and as citizens in the use of our economic resources. We have also looked at some of the ways in which we can begin to bring about change—as individuals and in cooperation with others. Now it is time to look at the possibilities for change from another perspective. Perhaps we shall be able to find guidance by examining quite a different approach to the problem.

Many, young people in particular, are trying to work out an alternative way of life to the "consumerism" which seems to trap so many of us. If you have ever ventured into the world of the counter culture or have had a conversation with a Consciousness III student, you may have had a rather uncomfortable experience. But if you got beyond your initial annoyance, you may have found yourself experiencing some feeling of appreciation for the best elements of the counter culture.[1]

Young radicals and other members of the activist counter culture are refusing to fit in with typical patterns of work, consumption, and sociability precisely because they *do* believe in the values their parents taught them, and they take these values seriously and want to live up to them. They refuse to get onto the treadmill of "consumerism" because they don't believe that happiness requires having all of the material possessions the ads encourage us to buy. They are not impressed with the symbols of status that cause many of us to show deference to high rank. They don't like to engage in small talk because they want greater significance in conversations and greater honesty and warmth in interpersonal relationships. Most of those who lay bodies on the line in protest actions against war and racial discrimination do so, not because they are intolerant of all authority and must show their independence to satisfy inner psychic needs, but because they really *care* about injustice and are willing to risk bodily injury and imprisonment in fighting against it. They refuse to be submissive students or unquestioning employees not because they are lazy, but because they do not want to be as blind as their teachers nor as enmeshed in fraud and oppression as their fathers and mothers.[2]

Do any of these actions perhaps challenge us to reexamine the goals and patterns of our own lives? How many of us are

[1] The terms "counter culture" and "Consciousness III" come from two widely acclaimed books on young people who have turned their backs on technological civilization. These books are Theodore Roszak's *The Making of a Counter Culture* (Garden City, N.Y.: Doubleday & Company, Inc., 1969) and Charles Reich's *The Greening of America* (New York: Random House, Inc., 1970).

[2] Kenneth Keniston, *Young Radicals: Notes on Committed Youth* (New York: Harcourt, Brace Jovanovich, Inc., 1968), pp. 44-76.

so convinced of the rightness and worthiness of our jobs that
we can cast a stone at those whose sense of integrity keeps
them from accepting one like it? How many of us are so
liberated from false pride of status that we can rebuke those
who scorn it? How many of us are so completely
uncontaminated by the desire for more and more material
things that we can poke fun at those who seek a less cluttered,
less frantic life? How many of us have worked so bravely and
wisely for justice that we can say with certainty, "Your way
of struggling for righteousness doesn't work as well as
ours"?

Could it be that the counter culture has at least some
manifestation of health as well as sickness? Could it be that
Consciousness III individuals are saying something
important about the dishonesty and the inequity of our age
that we should be hearing? Even though their vision is often
clouded by romantic illusions or even the false lights of
drugs, it is thought by some to be a contemporary rediscovery
of a vision of human sanity, fulfillment, and brotherhood
that is very much in accord with biblical faith. Could it be
that this viewpoint does present some challenge to some of
our long-established goals? Are too many of us pretty
thoroughly mired down in a very unchristian pattern of
economic activities and attitudes?

Economic folly and injustice probably cannot be
overcome without a new perspective on the good life which
emphasizes reverence for and relatedness to nature instead of
mastery over nature and exploitation of it. The sort of
breakthrough that we need is the awareness that *deliverance
from the yoke of "consumerism" is a gift of grace which we
must accept and affirm for the sake of our own freedom and
fulfillment as well as for the sake of justice in the human
community.*

Only by coming to have a lively sense of the amusing futility of our pathetic pursuit of happiness through buying can we be free to cultivate our capacities for genuine joy and love. Only by being able to laugh and shout, "Who needs it?" can we have a healthy enjoyment of prosperity instead of nervous bondage to its imperious demands. Only by ceasing to think of sharing as a burden and coming to see it as a free expression of the abundance of grace granted to us in Christ can we fulfill our responsibilities to others, and only thus can we fulfill our own nature as beings who are meant for covenant community with them.

If we really want to be free of the yoke of "consumerism," perhaps we should explore a new sort of *Christian asceticism*, a revolution in consciousness that will make the conscience of the Christian more responsive than it usually has been. Here are some of the details of this transformed style of life implied by a transformation of consciousness:

• There is *no need to practice renunciation of all material and technological goods* just because they are modern, or simply for the sake of giving them up. Unless one has a very special spiritual vocation, there is no particular nobility in that kind of sacrifice. What we need is wisdom, a perspective, a skill in living with material things and not allowing them to become the master of life. The purpose of renunciation is to get rid of the choking underbrush that robs us of both ethical vitality and true fulfillment, to free our resources of money, time, and intelligence for genuinely worthwhile activities.

If one abandons a certain job, or quits responding to certain kinds of advertising bait, or starts collecting books for a ghetto school instead of moonlighting to buy a motorboat, he is *not really making a sacrifice* if he is motivated by a free consciousness. He isn't sacrificing if he is acting out of a desire to fulfill his destiny as co-creator with God of a more humane society.

To gain a whole world of material comforts and conveniences at the price of losing our souls is *crazy*—no intelligent human being in his right mind and in a state of grace would do such a thing. This is not self-denial, really; it is true self-fulfillment. The yoke of deliverance from "consumerism" is easy and light; only a fool would prefer enslavement to Mammon and his array of spurious goods (Matthew 6:24; 10:39; 11:30).

• The new asceticism appropriate to Christians in the technologically advanced nations is significantly new in its pragmatic discrimination between the *genuine benefits* of such things as electricity, the automobile, the mass media on the one hand, and on the other hand, *meaningless or destructive uses* of these things. Given the need to cut back on consumption of electric energy and the need to reduce the pollution of the atmosphere caused by the internal combustion engine, it is the better part of wisdom to disengage ourselves from excessive dependence on these things for both ethical and ecological reasons.

For example, some people would say we can have electric lights, a stove, and a refrigerator without having air-conditioning, a freezer, a power saw, and a number of other items which are not strictly necessary, or are inefficient in terms of purchase and exclusive use. We can do more walking, cycling, and car-pooling and work as hard as we can for good public transportation, without giving up the use of automobiles entirely. We can refuse to buy expensively gadgeted new cars and wait for the engineers to come up with something more sensible. We can use the mass media intelligently for education or relaxation without losing our souls to them.

• We won't have to take vows of extreme poverty, chastity, and obedience in the new asceticism. But we do have to commit ourselves to some very *specific readjustments in our ways of living.* This could begin with recognizing that a job or a career choice is not smart if it is made purely for maximum financial return. A sense of fulfillment in a vocation ordained by God is more important, and so is an ethical evaluation of the output and the quality of life in the firm and the line of work with which you associate yourself.

The Christian ascetic will not define success in life in terms of a steadily growing accumulation of property, possessions, and paper assets. Taxes which are going to be used to promote human welfare will be accepted gladly, but the waste of tax money should always be protested. Charitable contributions will not be given grudgingly. They will be affirmed as a way to express solidarity with the great community of all life on which we depend for sustenance.

• The new Christian asceticism leads to a solid inner preference for investment of time and energy in *truly warm and joyful sharing* of oneself with other persons, or in constructive endeavors for a better community and world. It leads to the surrender of all expectations and desires for a life that is easy or riskless. So long as the demons of poverty, sickness, and sin ravage the earth, the Christian should never even *want* to escape to an island of noninvolvement. He will welcome his destiny as a co-worker with God in the struggle for righteousness.

If we really understand rebirth in Christ—the *new being* that is God's gracious gift through him—we know that a life of caring and sharing and laboring in the vineyard of the Lord is a joyous privilege, not a burden. "If any one has the world's goods and sees his brother in need, yet closes his heart against him, how does God's love abide in him?" (1

John 2:17). If we are able to live in selfish comfort, and if we have been so thoroughly brainwashed by technological, consumer culture as to think that this kind of "good" life is successful and happy, then, in truth, the love of God is not in us. And without the riches of his spirit, we have nothing and are nothing.

A TIME FOR DECISION

And now comes the biggest experiment of all—the hour of decision. It's time now to commit yourself on some of the issues raised in this book. You've probably been exposed to a lot of new information and ideas. What is going to be your response in changed attitudes or actions?

Probably every reader will agree that there are several life-styles, not just one, which can be rewarding in the best sense, responsible to others, and truly Christian. But we must all choose some life-style. What will that be? No one can make that decision for you; it is yours alone.

Perhaps the best way to conclude this book is to leave you with some unanswered questions:

Are you really serious about wanting to lead a dedicated Christian life, if only someone would show you the way?

Do you really want to change your life significantly, or do you prefer to sit tight and not rock the boat of the status quo?

Do you recognize that while economic reforms are needed you wanted them to come without any real inconvenience or discomfort to you?

What really is essential to you?

Do you so despair of ever accomplishing much change in the world that by your indifference, confusion, ineffectiveness, and inaction you won't even try to do what you can?

Some church people may find it hard to take seriously the idea of a drastic reorientation of personal aspirations and life-style. Yet that may be exactly what is called for if most of us are to fulfill our stewardship obligations in economic life.

What will YOU do?